FROM MY JEWEL BOX

Gladys Doonan

Gladys Doonan

Ps. 18:30 – 32

REGULAR BAPTIST PRESS
1300 North Meacham Road
Post Office Box 95500
Schaumburg, Illinois 60195

Library of Congress Cataloging in Publication Data

Doonan, Gladys, 1934–
    From my jewel box.

    1. Meditations.   2. Doonan, Gladys, 1934–
I. Title.
BV4832.2.D66   1983   248.4'861   83-4439
ISBN 0-87227-092-0

PREFACE

In the spring of 1977, a phone call came to me one day from Reverend Donald Brong, State Representative of the Iowa Association of Regular Baptist Churches. He inquired as to my interest in writing a regular monthly column for the *Iowa Regular Baptist,* state paper of the Association, which would be for and about the ladies in the churches of our fellowship. This was totally unexpected but was evidently planned for me by the Lord. Just such a project had been a dream of mine for a very long time.

I agreed, was informed about deadlines, length of copy and other necessary details, then took up my pen and began regularly producing "The Jewel Box." Its reception by our Iowa Regular Baptist ladies has been overwhelming. A whole new world of friendship and fellowship has opened up for me. I enjoy writing the column but, more important than that, writing has become a spiritual blessing to me. How wonderful, then, to receive telephone calls and letters (some even from the mission fields) that tell me it is being read and enjoyed and is blessing others as well. I praise the Lord! He is so good!

The pages of this little book contain selected articles taken from those published over the past four years. We began at the beginning so the material is in somewhat chronological order, though some months will be missing. Those included have been edited only slightly and they are now sent out to all the ladies of the GARBC and others who are interested with my prayer that hearts may be blessed and challenged through them.

I do regret that authors and sources have not always been available in quoting material taken from my personal scrapbooks. If copyrights have been violated in any case, it has been unintentional. I offer my personal thanks to all whose material has been used for the blessing it has been to me personally and also to our ladies.

I welcome your comments and suggestions concerning this ministry and will certainly answer any who write to me.

Gladys Doonan (Mrs. Michael Doonan)
1821 N.W. Fourth Street
Ankeny, Iowa 50021

Introduction

Many, many years ago in England, there lived a woman whose love for the Savior and beautifully consecrated life were an inspiration to all who knew her. About midnight February 4, 1874, following the thrilling experience of leading two souls to faith in Christ, she took her pen and wrote the words of a hymn we still sing in our churches today.

It began, "Take my life, and let it be consecrated, Lord, to Thee." After ten couplets of enumerating all the things she wanted the Lord to have, she closed with, "Take myself and I will be ever, only, all for Thee!"

Frances Ridley Havergal meant those words and proved them every day by the way she lived, always looking for something more she could do for her Savior. Four years after the hymn was penned, she wrote in a letter to a friend: "The Lord has shown me another little step, and of course I have taken it with extreme delight. 'Take my silver and my gold' now means shipping off all my ornaments to the Church Missionary House (including a jewel cabinet that is really fit for a countess), where all will be accepted and disposed of for me.

"I retain a brooch or two for daily wear, which are memorials of my dear parents, also a locket containing a

portrait of my dear niece in heaven and her two rings, but
these I redeem, so that the whole value goes to the
Church Missionary Society. Nearly fifty articles are being
packed up. I don't think I ever packed a box with such
pleasure."

Oh, that more of us today had that kind of dedication
to Christ and that kind of burden for His work! Would we
be willing to give up our dearest earthly possessions that
others might hear the gospel?

Probably not many of us have the kind of jewels
which, even if surrendered, would bring much in the way
of money to give toward missions. However, there is one
thing which all of us who know the Lord can do. We can
pray the prayer of Miss Havergal's hymn, "Take myself
and I will be ever, only, all for Thee!" Thus, we can give
ourselves to Him to use in any way He chooses for His
own glory.

Since God has said in His Word (Prov. 31:10) that the
price of a virtuous woman is "far above rubies," doesn't it
stand to reason that such a life, yielded to Him, would be
worth even more to Him than any jewels? Let us seek to
be all that He wants us to be as we serve Him.

I looked into my own jewelry box just the other day
and what I found was certainly not "fit for a countess"!
There is a tiny diamond ring, my birthstone, which my dad
bought for my eleventh birthday just a few months before
his death. There is a huge medallion on a tarnished chain
with a broken clasp which I wouldn't trade for any amount
of money. It was my very first gift, some twenty-five years
ago, from the one who is now my dear husband. There is
also the little string of pearls, a bit yellowed, which I wore
with my wedding dress the December night I became a
bride.

There's a hodge-podge of what we call "costume
jewelry," favorite pins and necklaces picked up here and
there at sales. My jewel box contains a little bit of

everything, just trinkets and ornaments of no real monetary worth but very precious to me in sentimental value.

I thought of this when Mr. Donald Brong, state representative of the Iowa Association of Regular Baptist Churches, made a very old dream come true the other day by asking me to write this monthly column for our state paper. He said to be sure to come up with a special name that would capture the attention of the women of our fellowship. Catchy or not, I couldn't get the "The Jewel Box" out of my mind, and that's what it's going to be.

This column is just for you, ladies, and it will contain, like my jewelry box, a little bit of everything. There will be TREASURES OF TRUTH, little GEMS OF INSPIRATION, hopefully some SPARKLING IDEAS for your missionary groups, and maybe even a GLEAM OF HUMOR now and then.

I've enjoyed our visit! Have you?

June

During the latter half of the nineteenth century, there lived a poet by the name of Edwin Hodder who contemplated the wonders of God's Word, the Bible, and wrote these beautiful lines concerning it.

> Thy Word is like a garden, Lord,
> With flowers bright and fair;
> And everyone who seeks may pluck
> A lovely cluster there.
>
> Thy Word is like a deep, deep mine;
> And jewels rich and rare
> Are hidden in its mighty depths
> For every searcher there.
>
> Thy Word is like a starry host:
> A thousand rays of light
> Are seen to guide the traveler,
> And make his pathway bright.
>
> Thy Word is like an armory
> Where soldiers may repair,
> And find for life's long battle day
> All needful weapons there.

O may I love Thy precious Word,
May I explore the mine,
May I its fragrant flowers glean,
May light upon me shine.

O may I find my armor there,
The Word my trusty sword;
I'll learn to fight with every foe
The battle of the Lord.

Flowers! Jewels! Light! Armor! These words and scores of others poetically describe the treasures of truth the Christian finds in God's wonderful Book. How thankful we should be that He has blessed us with His Word!

I particularly appreciate the simile likening the Bible to a mine filled with hidden jewels, to make rich any and all who care to seek them out. I've found some! Have you?

Have you ever been studying the Bible when suddenly a certain verse would shine out and glow with new meaning and beauty, just as a gem shines out and glows when light strikes its many facets? Or, has a friend ever come to you in trying circumstances to share a portion of Scripture which just exactly fits your case? You reached out eagerly to grasp it and possess it as your own, just as you would desire to possess a rare and precious stone.

In March of 1977, all of my well-made plans had to suddenly and unexpectedly be set aside as I entered the hospital for major surgery. A very special Christian friend came to me with Joshua 1:9. I read the words again and again. I committed them to memory. They gleamed and sparkled in my mind with the clear beauty of diamonds. What a blessing it was to go into the operating room remembering that the Lord was with me, even there!

Many of you reading this may have health problems. Perhaps you, too, face surgery. I pass on, especially to you, this jewel from the mine of God's Word. May it be as

precious to you in days to come as it has been to me in
days just past.

"Have not I commanded thee? Be strong and of a good
courage; be not afraid, neither be thou dismayed: for
the LORD thy God is with thee
whithersoever thou goest" (Joshua 1:9).

September

When I was just a little girl (many years ago!), one of my very favorite things to do was to get out the big, old-fashioned scrapbook kept diligently by my mother. I loved to leaf through its pages, reading and re-reading newspaper clippings, poems, clever sayings and anything else of interest she had come across in her reading.

I was fascinated by a little "optical illusion" she had pasted on one page which looked like a Grecian urn until you blinked your eyes; then you could see clearly that it was the profile of two women in silhouette facing one another. Blink again and the urn was back—the space between the two identical faces.

Time and again, I also read bits of verse written by my father before he died the year I turned eleven. One afternoon I even propped that book open on the end of the ironing board where I was working and memorized from it that beloved and meaningful poem, "The Touch of the Master's Hand." I can still quote it to this day.

At sixty-five years of age, my mother is still "clipping," still keeping scrapbooks. Because of her example, I am also a scrapbook-keeper. I love to sit down with one of my own nowadays and be blessed again by things I have pasted there.

I'm sure some of those things would be a blessing to you, so this time our JEWEL BOX is going to contain "Gems of Truth" from the pages of my scrapbooks.

STRIVE ALWAYS TO BE LIKE A GOOD WATCH—
open face, busy hands, pure gold, well regulated,
full of good works.

———

Look back and thank God for His grace,
Look up with trust into His face,
Look on with hope to future days,
Look unto Him and give Him praise!

———

WE SHOULDN'T JUST SPEND TIME . . .
WE SHOULD INVEST IT!

Did you know that your heart, if normal, beats approximately 100,000 times each day, a million times every ten days and between thirty-six and thirty-eight million times every year? Every hour your heart expends enough energy to carry a 150-pound man from street level to the top of a three-story building. Every day it pushes from five to ten tons of blood (depending on your body size) through your blood vessels. If you reach your allotted three-score years and ten, your heart, in those seventy years, will have exerted enough force to lift the world's largest battleship fourteen feet out of the water. You are "fearfully and wonderfully made!"

The Lord Jesus is still praying . . .
He ever lives to pray us through.
30 years of living on earth . . .
3 years of serving . . .
1 tremendous act of dying . . .
1900 YEARS OF PRAYING!

What an emphasis on prayer!

It is God's will that I should cast
My care on Him each day (*1 Pet. 5:7*);
He also asks me not to cast
My confidence away (*Heb. 10:35*).
But, oh, how stupidly I act
When taken unaware . . .
I cast away my confidence,
And carry all my care!
— *T. Baird*

If I'm to be a Martha, Lord,
I surely want to be
A Martha with a Mary-heart
That listens well to Thee.
And as each hour passes by
In work for those I love,
Dear Lord, be whispering to me
About the things Above.
An alabaster box of praise,
A moment at Thy feet,
Can change the dreariest day to one
Where even chores are sweet.
So, help me honor Thee as Guest
And choose the better part . . .
I'll gladly be a Martha, Lord,
But give me Mary's heart!
— *R. G. Zwall*

I hope these little "treasures" of mine have been a blessing and have given you something to think about.

October

A familiar little song sung by the children in our churches is entitled, "When He Cometh," and has to do with that day when the Lord comes to "make up [His] jewels" (Mal. 3:17). The last stanza of the song begins with these words: "Little children, little children who love their Redeemer, are the jewels, precious jewels, His loved and His own."

I thought of that song recently when one of the Vacation Bible School teachers from our church stopped to chat a moment in the grocery store and tell of her work with the beginners. Before presenting the lesson story that day, she had said words to this effect: "Boys and girls, it is time to pray now. Let's bow our heads and close our eyes and ask the Lord Jesus to be with us and help us and open our hearts so we can learn what He wants us to know."

The little heads were bowed, the little eyes were closed, and the teacher prayed for the Lord's blessing. However, the wording of her prayer was just a little different from her introduction. When she finished, a little four-year-old piped up with, "Teacher, you forgot to say 'open our hearts'!"

Ladies, isn't it a precious privilege to give the sweet gospel story of God's love to the eager, responsive little "jewels" in our churches? I don't deny that they can be naughty and even exasperating sometimes, but what potential is wrapped up in little lives! When you're tempted to despair and give up, think of these meaningful words from an unknown poet:

> A diamond in the rough
> Is a diamond, sure enough,
> For before it ever sparkled
> It was made of diamond stuff.
> Of course, someone must find it,
> Or it never will be found.
> And then, someone must grind it,
> Or it never will be ground.
> But when it's found and when it's ground
> And when it's burnished bright,
> That diamond's everlastingly
> Flashing out its radiant light.
> O, Teacher, please, whoe'er you be,
> Don't say you've done enough.
> That worst child in your class may be
> A diamond in the rough!

★　★　★　★　★　★

One sweet friend who has been a blessing and inspiration in my life recently wrote me a thank-you note for a ride to a ladies' retreat. These words from her letter were special to me. In speaking of her busy days . . .

"Well, it's true that not *every* moment has been devoted to work. Do you recall that bit of verse about buying 'hyacinths to feed the soul?' So, I have taken time to arrange marigolds in a freshly polished copper bowl with a candle in the center, to appreciate the hominess of smoke drifting from a neighbor's fire, to

delight in the smell of little girls' freshly shampooed
hair. My work, the 'routine things,' could become
drudgery, were it not for love . . . and things like these
to enjoy!"

How about you? What have you taken time to enjoy
today that has taken the drudgery from your busy-ness?

November

This morning as I sit down at my desk to visit with you for a few moments, the sky is gray and a slow drizzle is falling. Most of the bright and beautiful autumn leaves on display the past few weeks have fallen from the trees now and there is a decided edge to the wind that says clearly, "Winter is on its way!"

Tomorrow is November 1 and November means Thanksgiving. It's time for us to be busy counting our blessings. As I look back over the past year, I think I might run out of numbers. How about you? God is so good to us! We can surely echo a heartfelt "Amen!" to the words of the psalmist who wrote, "Blessed be the Lord, who daily loadeth us with benefits, even the God of our salvation" (Ps. 68:19).

Gleaming brightly, like choice jewels in the necklace of my year, are the friends the Lord has given to me . . . "old friends, new friends, tried and true friends" . . . friends who have prayed for me and with me and given me good counsel . . . friends who have shared my joys and my sorrows . . . friends who have given a smile or word of encouragement just when it was needed most . . . friends who have helped with the work and lightened the load . . . FRIENDS, A WONDERFUL GIFT FROM GOD!

This year I'm not going to let Thanksgiving go by without thanking my friends as well as thanking God for them. A pretty card with a few personal words of gratitude can mean a great deal. And you know what? Your friends might be blessed if you would do this, too!

Speaking of Thanksgiving . . . I've noticed that the produce departments of our grocery stores now have cranberries in stock again. My Aunt Minnie, who lives in Albuquerque, New Mexico, wrote me of a new and unusual and yummy way to use them. Let me give you the recipe.

CRANBERRY PIE

Grease a pie plate or 8-9 inch square baking dish with oleo. Place in this cranberries which have been washed and dried (2-3 cups for a pie plate; 4 cups for a deep dish).

Sprinkle over the berries: ½ cup sugar and ½ cup nuts. Mix: 2 eggs, ¼ cup cooking oil, 1 stick soft oleo, 1 cup flour, and 1 cup sugar. Spread this mixture carefully over the berries. Bake one hour at 325 degrees.

I've tried this and it is DELICIOUS!

★　★　★　★　★　★

Heaven has become a little bit dearer to me this past month. Let me tell you why.

The call came to our house at 4:45 A.M. on Monday, October 3. It was my sister-in-law, Kay, calling from Alamosa, Colorado, to tell me my brother had died at 2:30 A.M. Roy, who had his fortieth birthday in August, had been battling Hodgkins disease (cancer of the lymph system) for a little over two years. Now, the battle is over. Roy is with the Lord! How wonderful it is that God's Word is so very clear on this matter! For the Christian, "absent from the body . . . present with the Lord" (2 Cor. 5:8).

That evening, out on the highway somewhere near North Platte, Nebraska, on our way to the funeral, Mike

and I saw a breathtakingly beautiful sunset. We spoke of
the splendors Roy must be seeing and it suddenly struck
me that he was all done with sunsets. He is "at Home"
now, in the land of endless day—no more night, no more
suffering and pain, no more death! That thought was a
blessing to me, and I knew it would be to Kay as well. So
there in the car as we drove along, I wrote a poem for her
which was later read at Roy's funeral. I thought perhaps it
might be a blessing to you, too, as you think of your loved
ones who are already with the Lord.

> Beyond the bright horizon to the North,
> And out beyond the blueness of the sky,
> There lies the splendid city of our God
> Where saints are called to dwell with Him on high.
>
> And one, but lately passed to that fair place,
> Now done with all of suffering and pain,
> Looks round about with wonder and surprise
> And senses not Earth's loss—just his own gain!
>
> He sees the clear, transparent streets of gold,
> And gleam of gems now dazzles on his sight;
> He knows that every shimmering beauty there
> But lends its radiance from a borrowed Light.
>
> For years ago, in his own darkened heart,
> The true Light shined—his sins were all forgiven—
> And Christ, the Lamb of God, Who saved him then
> Is all the Light that's needed in God's Heaven.
>
> His voice this day is joined in songs of praise
> That yet shall echo through eternity.
> He is content to be, at last, "at Home"—
> That Home where he forevermore shall be.
>
> The sun is setting here on saddened hearts,
> But ne'er again a sunset shall he know;
> And sometime, in the day that shall not end,
> We'll join him and rejoice that it was so!

January

January 1 dawned cold and clear upon what our pastor called a "beautiful winter wonderland of snow." After the fierce blizzard of the night before, when huge drifts were piled high and then delicately sculpted by the skillful hand of the northeast wind, the world looked new and pure and unspoiled—just like the New Year which we faced that day.

I love the snow—have always loved it—and it never fails to remind me of that reassuring truth found in Isaiah 1:18, "Come now, and let us reason together, saith the LORD: though your sins be as scarlet, they shall be as white as snow. . . ." And right there at the gate to the New Year, I found myself echoing the heart cry of the psalmist, ". . . wash me, and I shall be whiter than snow" (Ps. 51:7).

Is it with you as it is with me? No matter how much progress I seem to make in a year, a new year always finds me realizing how far short I have fallen and wanting to make things different in the unspoiled days to come. Let's pray for one another faithfully, that the new year may find us attaining more fully unto what Christ would have us to be!

Just a little over a hundred years ago, at a beautiful estate in England called Winterdyne, set among the oaks

and beeches, the elms and sycamores of the woods
above the winding valley of the silvery Severn River, a
gentle and cultured Englishwoman mused by a fireside.
She was counting the blessings of the year just past and
wondering what future days might hold for her. Her
thoughts, as they so often did, took the form of verse and
Frances Ridley Havergal penned the words of a lovely
poem which is still used today as a hymn for New Year's
time. May these words be our prayer for our new year as
they were hers for 1874:

Another year is dawning!
Dear Master, let it be,
In working or in waiting,
Another year with Thee.

Another year of leaning
Upon Thy loving breast,
Of ever-deepening trustfulness,
Of quiet, happy rest.

Another year of mercies,
Of faithfulness and grace;
Another year of gladness
In the shining of Thy face.

Another year of progress,
Another year of praise;
Another year of proving
Thy presence "all the days."

Another year of service,
Of witness for Thy love;
Another year of training
For holier work above.

Another year is dawning!
Dear Master, let it be,
On earth, or else in Heaven
Another year for Thee!

The new year offers us twelve months or 365 days or 8,760 hours or 525,600 minutes or 31,536,000 seconds in which to live for and serve the Lord. May we treasure each precious measure of time as a choice jewel! May we realize its value! May we make it count for eternity!

★ ★ ★ ★ ★ ★

I know that many of you ladies are busy right now with committee meetings and planning the activities for your ladies' groups in the new year.

Why not plan one of your evening meetings as "Men's Night," with your husbands (and all men of the church) as your honored guests. Use a missionary couple as speakers. Why not ask each man to bring a man's item for your missionary cupboard? They'll stock your cupboard with useful things for the missionary men which you might never think of. We have used this idea in our own church with great success and many appreciative comments afterward.

Another idea—combine prayer with work at one of your project meetings. Set a loud alarm clock for well-spaced intervals. Whenever it goes off, have everyone stop, share requests for your missionaries and have a brief time of prayer.

Is your ladies' group a large one from a large church? Why not encourage the ladies' group from a small or struggling church by inviting them to join you as special guests at one of your regular meetings? This could be a real blessing and give a real boost to their work.

February

During the last week, we have had a young woman from Michigan visiting in our home. A dear friend since she was about eight years old, she has without a doubt one of the prettiest smiles of anyone I know. Her dimples deepen; her eyes sparkle; her whole face lights up—and people feel like smiling back.

The smile of one we love is a precious thing—a very special kind of treasure. And a smile from almost anyone—friend or stranger—can encourage our hearts and brighten our days.

An Oakland, California, newspaper of several years ago carried the story of an elderly patient in the county hospital. Anne, as she was affectionately called by staff and fellow-patients, was then almost eighty and had been a resident there for several years. She was somewhat of a philosopher and spent her days moving slowly up and down the halls, in and out of the rooms, cheering the despondent and those whom she felt were physically worse off than she was.

The doctors would watch Anne hobbling painfully about on her crutches and shake their heads in amazement at her unfailing fortitude. A physician turned to his nurse one day and said, "The remarkable thing about her is her smile, for it stays, no matter how ill she may be or how intense her suffering is."

He mentioned this in the old woman's presence, too, and asked her if she thought smiling made a sick person feel better. She looked up alertly and shook her head as she replied, "No, it doesn't make you feel any better to smile when you're sick, but think how much better other people will think you feel. That makes them feel better, and it's a good thing to make somebody else feel better!"

Ladies, we Christians, of all people on earth, have more reason to be happy and express that joy to others by a smile than anyone else. Sins forgiven! The sure hope of eternity in Heaven with our Savior! Precious promises of strength for each day and the supply of every need! God's Word to nourish and bless us! The great privilege of living for and loving the Lord!

These priceless blessings, realized and appreciated, can fill our lives to overflowing with happiness and make us, like Anne, delight in making somebody else feel better. A sincere smile, a word of cheer or sharing the good news of the gospel can mean so much to a lonely sin-sick soul!

One of the greatest ministries a Christian can have is to encourage others—not only the unsaved but brothers and sisters in Christ as well. As we look at those about us, we need to ask the Lord to make us sensitive to their needs. Then we should do our part in helping to meet those needs.

Many hundreds of years ago, there lived a man who was also an overcomer in the face of trying circumstances. His name was Paul. In spite of all kinds of trials and hard experiences in his life, he remained cheerful and more concerned about others than himself. He treasured the grace of God as a precious jewel and found it abundantly sufficient in every situation.

Through the centuries, thousands of saints have been blessed and encouraged by his attitude. He declared, "I take pleasure in infirmities, in reproaches, in necessities, in persecutions, in distresses for Christ's sake: for when I am weak, then am I strong" (2 Cor. 12:10).

How do you meet trying circumstances? Have you encouraged anyone else today? Are you smiling?

March

Just lately I have been thinking about a different kind of "jewel" than usual. It is a new afghan pattern (new to me, at least!) called the Indian Diamond. The sample was beautiful and, though I didn't think I could do it, I bought yarn in four shades of green and boldly began. It's not as hard as I expected and is so much fun I can't leave it alone—I'm already over two-thirds finished!

This pattern has a special stitch every so often called a "double crochet drop." Done correctly, this periodic simple maneuver of the hook forms a lovely design of raised diamonds covering the whole afghan. By sad experience I learned that just one little "bump" left out or misplaced could ruin all I was trying to do, spoiling the design and marring the pattern.

As I sat painstakingly raveling out my work one day to correct such a mistake, I began to think about the similarities of crocheting an afghan and the Christian life. Really, it's very much the same. As long as I follow closely the pattern given in God's Word, all is well and my life can be used of Him to show His grace to others. But just let me leave out a needed "stitch" such as Bible study or prayer, or let me add an unneeded "stitch" such as pride or grumbling, and the whole design is spoiled. My testimony is marred and ineffective.

My little story is a reminder to all of us (myself included!) that we need to "count stitches" carefully, closely following God's pattern that our lives might be beautiful to His glory and a witness to the world.

By the way, ladies, have you written to your missionaries lately? I know it takes time (and there seems to be a shortage of that!), but what a blessed ministry it can be, for you and to them.

Several years ago I prepared for the ladies of our church a sheet of tips on writing to missionaries. Many expressed appreciation, and I reprint it here for you with the prayer that it may result in some mail for our missionaries around the world.

LET'S WRITE TO OUR MISSIONARIES!

You've never met them? You don't know what to say? Remember, missionaries are people like you, interested in the same types of things you are. The following tips may help you get started.

1. ENCOURAGEMENT—Just taking the time from your busy schedule to let your missionaries know you're thinking of them will bring them a blessing. If you don't have time for a long letter, write a short one!

2. ASSURANCE OF PRAYER SUPPORT—Your missionaries count on your prayers as they serve the Lord day by day. They like to hear that you really are praying!

3. TESTIMONY OF BLESSING—Perhaps a certain portion of Scripture has spoken to you in recent days. Share this! Perhaps you have had an exciting answer to prayer. Share this! Perhaps your heart is filled with praise for the Lord's working in your life. Share this! Perhaps you've had a thrilling opportunity to witness. Share this!

30

4. PERSONAL NEWS—Let your missionaries get to know you and your family by sharing with them some little "homey" experience of everyday life—the cake that fell, vacation plans, burdens and blessings concerning your children, a good book you've read lately. Enclose a snapshot. Let other family members add a line or two to your letter!

5. CHURCH NEWS—Since your church supports these missionaries, they have a special interest in your church. Keep them up to date on staff changes, youth activities, special meetings, guest speakers, musical blessings, decisions made, the Lord's leading and prospering of your group. They'll even appreciate notes of the pastor's latest sermon. Introduce new members to them by mail—ask a new member to add a few lines to your letter. If a missionary is personally acquainted with your church people, he will want details of weddings, births, deaths, graduations, illnesses, etc. Your church bulletin sent regularly could be a blessing, too!

6. PRAYER LETTERS—Sometimes an especially exciting prayer letter from one missionary can be a blessing when sent to another. Your own message should be written on the back!

7. SPECIAL GROUPS—If you have an active Campus Bible Fellowship work in your area, or Awana or Joy Clubs, your missionaries would appreciate knowing how the Lord is using these ministries!

8. HUMOR AND INSPIRATION—Have you heard a good joke lately or a clever saying or read an inspirational poem? Share these and brighten your missionary's day!

One last tip—WRITE OFTEN! You know how it strengthens your faith to hear of God's blessings in your missionaries' lives? Well, it works in the other direction, too; their faith is strengthened when they hear of God's working in your life. You know how much you appreciate their specific prayer requests so you can pray for them intelligently? Well, it also works in the other direction; they appreciate your specific prayer requests so they can pray for you intelligently.

Writing to the missionaries can be a ministry blessed of the Lord. How about it? Will you have a part?

April

Many years ago, the story was told of a small shepherd boy who longed to know God and talk to Him, but he did not know how. He had heard that God was the One Who made the earth and everything in it so day by day, as he cared for his sheep on the hilly fields, he would look about him at God's beautiful creation and consider with wonder the greatness of such a Being. He studied the animals and birds, he thought about the marvels of his own body, and he was awed by the wisdom of such a Being. But no one came to tell him about God's love for him and no one taught him to pray.

Every Sunday morning the little shepherd boy would sit high on the hillside and listen to the melodious sound of the church bells ringing out across the valley. Then he would watch as the carriages rolled slowly down the road to the churchyard and people (just tiny specks in the distance) climbed the church steps and went through the door. How he wished that he might go to church, too, and learn about God! But he would look down at his ragged clothes and his bare feet and somehow feel that he might not be welcomed there. Besides, he had to care for his sheep.

One particular Sunday morning he led his flock down the hillside and nearer to the road. The bells were chiming in the sweet spring air and he felt, rather foolishly perhaps, that getting nearer the bells, nearer the church, would get him nearer God. As the sheep grazed on the lush green grass that grew in the lowlands, he wandered idly toward the hedge that bordered the field and stood there listening longingly.

Suddenly the little shepherd boy was overwhelmed by his spiritual need. No matter that he did not know how to pray! He simply had to talk to God! He dropped to his knees, bowed his head and closed his eyes. Then, in a hushed and reverent voice, he began slowly repeating the alphabet—A, B, C, D . . . right on toward Z!

A deacon from the church with the bells, an old man with white hair and a kindly face, was hurrying along the road at just that moment. He was rushed because he was late for services. His horse had thrown a shoe and he had been forced to walk into town. Now he stopped and held up a hand to his ear. What was that? He thought he heard a voice—yes! There it was again, on the other side of the hedge; a childish voice—who could it be?

With no regard for the trousers his wife had so carefully pressed or the shoes he had so carefully shined, he plunged across the ditch, gingerly parted the thorny branches of the hedge and looked through. He was amazed to see a small boy on his knees in an attitude of prayer and completely unaware of his presence. And what was that the boy was saying? His ABCs! In his surprise the old man exclaimed, "I say, little man, what are you doing?"

The lad, startled, jumped to his feet and stammered, "I . . . I . . . please, sir, I was only praying."

The old man's eyes widened. "Praying?" he repeated. "Praying? But it sounded like you were saying your letters."

The shepherd boy hung his head sheepishly, then answered slowly, "Well, you see, sir, I don't know how to pray. I've never done it before. But today I felt like I just had to talk to God. I wanted Him to be with me and take care of me and help me take good care of my sheep . . . only . . . well, I didn't know how to tell Him. Someone told me one time that God knows all about us, so I thought if I would just say my letters . . . since God knows all about me . . . He would understand and He could spell it all out the right way Himself!"

The old deacon was touched by the boy's simple faith and he replied in a trembling voice, "Well, bless your heart, little man! He will! He will! He will!"

This simple story from the past reminds us of some precious verses in God's Word that shine out to us with jewel-like brilliance. Romans 8:26 and 27 say to the needy, troubled heart, "Likewise the Spirit also helpeth our infirmities: for we know not what we should pray for as we ought: but the Spirit itself maketh intercession for us with groanings which cannot be uttered. And he that searcheth the hearts knoweth what is the mind of the Spirit, because he maketh intercession for the saints according to the will of God."

Ladies, most of us have gone to church all our lives. We know God in a living, vital way through faith in His Son. We have been taught to pray and talking to God is as natural for us as talking to our loved ones. Yet, are there not many times when our need is so great and our lives so unworthy that we come to the Lord in prayer but "know not what we should pray for as we ought"? How precious, then, to realize that God Himself, in the Person of the Holy Spirit, knows and understands the deepest longings of our hearts and takes our inadequate words and "spells it all out the right way Himself!"

May

Written on the little maple-framed chalkboard in my kitchen are two words—THINK SPRING! They were printed there on one of those peevish, blustery cold days when the calendar said it should be spring but the weatherman said it wasn't. However, that advice is no longer needed; just a peek out my window gives the same message loud and clear.

There's the blushing beauty of blossoming trees blending with the bright tints of the tulips. There's the vivid royal hue of tiny grape hyacinths in contrast to the sunshine shades of graceful, slender daffodils. There's grass so radiantly green it almost hurts our winter-weary eyes. There's the delicate, honey-sweet fragrance which hovers in the new-warm air and stirs with every passing breeze. There's bird-song and bee-hum and the resurrection excitement of new life bursting forth on every side. SPRINGTIME!

We live on a corner lot in Ankeny, Iowa, just across the street from Faith Baptist Bible College where my husband teaches music. Should you happen by our place some sunny day this summer, Mike will be sure to give you the "grand tour" of our yard. You might be amazed to see thirteen apple trees, three peach trees, three apricot trees, three plum trees, a cherry tree, a pear tree, a dozen hazelnut bushes, sixteen varieties of grapes, plus various other kinds of greenery too numerous to mention. And wouldn't you know it? Just today a little almond tree and three more grapevines arrived in the mail!

Is our yard full? Well—yes, it is, and getting fuller all the time. But there is an empty spot this spring that wasn't there last summer. It's the place behind the garage where for five years a red Caco grapevine has grown and flourished.

It was a beautiful vine which sent out long healthy branches in every direction and which was covered with huge, green leaves and curling tendrils. Just one thing was wrong—that Caco never bore grapes! Each February it was carefully pruned. Each spring we eagerly watched for signs of fruit forming, but always in vain. And this year judgment fell upon it. Mike said, "If that vine isn't going to bear grapes, it has to go!" Then he mercilessly cut it down and planned for a more fruitful vine to take its place.

The whole incident reminded me of John 15 where Jesus said to His followers, "I am the true vine, and my Father is the husbandman. Every branch in me that beareth not fruit he taketh away. . . ." Ladies, we are to be fruit-bearing Christians.

Let us produce more than just "leaves" for our Master. Our lives should be filled with the "fruit of the Spirit" spoken of in Galatians 5 (*love, joy, peace, long-suffering, gentleness, goodness, faith, meekness, temperance*) so that we might be effective witnesses pointing unsaved souls to Christ.

An unknown author has pointed out the importance of the testimony of our lives in this thought-provoking poem:

> I am my neighbor's Bible,
> He reads me when we meet;

Today He reads me in my home,
Tomorrow in the street.
He may be relative or friend,
Or slight acquaintance be;
He may not even know my name,
Yet he is reading me.

And pray, who is this neighbor
Who reads me day by day,
To learn if I am living right
And walking as I pray?
Yes, he is ever watching
To criticize or blame;
So worldly-wise in his own eyes—
And "Sinner" is his name.

Dear Christian friends, we solely need
To realize each day
How carefully the world observes
Just what we do and say!
Then we must write our record plain
That in time we might see
That worldly neighbor won to Christ
And from his sin set free.

This is your "gem" from the JEWEL BOX today.

June

Willard J. Funk—poet, lexicographer and president of Funk and Wagnalls Publishing Company—once listed what he considered to be the ten most beautiful words in the English language. They were chosen, he explained, because of their meaning and musical arrangement of the letters from which they are formed. Here is his list:

1. dawn
2. hush
3. lullaby
4. murmuring
5. tranquil
6. mist
7. luminous
8. chimes
9. golden
10. melody

Almost everyone would agree that these words are, indeed, beautiful; the simple reading of the list calls to mind many an appealing image. They would seem to lend truth to the expression of the poet:

> God wove a web of loveliness
> Of clouds and stars and birds,
> But made not anything at all
> So beautiful as words.

Even though we Christians might agree upon the

obvious beauty of the words from Mr. Funk's list, were we asked to set down our own "top ten," our choices would probably be altogether different. It is likely that we would not consider the musical arrangement of letters at all, but turn our thoughts to the spiritual and base our decision on meaning alone. We would think of words like Savior, love, grace, forgiveness, joy, peace, Heaven. . . .

Say, what to you are the ten most beautiful words?

★　★　★　★　★　★

Each spring for the past several years, the Lord has given me the wonderful privilege of speaking at various mother-daughter events in churches in our state. This is always a delightful experience, and I never cease to be amazed at the clever ideas the ladies come up with for themes, programs and decorations.

At one church, for example, there was a Saturday morning brunch and a special highlight of that day was to have thirty-nine great-grandmothers in attendance. When we went to the fellowship hall for a delicious fruit cup, sweet rolls and coffee or tea after the program, we sat at tables cheerily decorated with live, blooming geranium plants. Every great-grandmother got to take a geranium home with her. What a lovely idea! Better file that one, ladies!

Then, at another church, I fellowshiped with the ladies and girls around the special theme, "A MOTHER'S JOB—SEVEN DAYS A WEEK." You guessed it—the tables for the salad buffet were decorated for the different days of the week and the decorations depicted mother's jobs. Things like scrub brushes, pots and pans, irons—very clever! And very attractive!

Ladies, I hope each of you has a blessed and beautiful summer. In the more relaxed atmosphere of vacation-time, don't forget the Lord and your

40

responsibilities to Him. And wherever you go or whatever you're doing, let the truth of this little gem from our Jewel Box sparkle in your memory:

> He knows! He loves! He cares!
> Nothing this truth can dim—
> God gives the very best to those
> Who leave the choice with Him!

August

Many hundreds of years ago, David exclaimed to the Lord, "I will praise Thee; for I am fearfully and wonderfully made" (Ps. 139:14).

We can echo those words of the psalmist whenever we take time to consider the wonders of our physical bodies, particularly our hands. I want us to think about our hands for a few moments together.

Look at the hands which hold the paper before you. Did you realize that each of those hands is made up of twenty-seven different bones, thirty-five powerful muscles, a vast network of arteries and veins which circulate your blood through them to keep your hands warm and supple, plus countless nerves which carry messages between your hands and your brain? All of these vital parts have an incredibly thin, incredibly durable protective covering of skin.

Those two hands of yours, with at least four kinds of nerve endings, have the most sensitive and acute sense of touch in your entire body. Even with your eyes closed, your hands can tell you whether something is hot or cold, rough or smooth, soft or firm, slick or fuzzy. And that amazing sense of touch can be so highly developed that

42

blind people can read with the tips of their fingers by a
method known as Braille.

When you were just a tiny baby, you were unable to
do very much with your hands except wave them in the air
or suck on them. But with each passing month and year
you gained more control over them and learned to do
many new things—to reach out, to grasp, to hold things
securely, to feed yourself, to write and paint and play the
piano.

Now, as an adult, those hands of yours are two highly
specialized tools. Just think, ladies, of all the many, many
things you can do just because the Lord saw fit to give
you hands. Have you thanked Him for your hands lately?

You know, those hands of yours can serve the Lord,
too. How? By using whatever you hold in your hands for
Him. Remember the Old Testament story of Moses? One
day God said to him, "What is that in thine hand?" All
Moses held was a staff, but our God is so great that He
can use even a stick if the hand holding it is yielded to
Him!

One friend of mine wrote in regard to serving the
Lord, "Many times we ladies think that what we have or
what we are able to do isn't important. But here are some
things which, if you have them in your hand, you can use
to serve." Let's all profit from her suggestions.

1. The Bible and other Christian books—for our own
   help and the help of others when given as gifts.
2. The telephone—to show friendship and concern for
   others and to invite others to church.
3. A pen—for writing letters to missionaries.
4. Prayer letters—to read and then pray earnestly for
   needs mentioned.
5. Sewing—to meet the needs of others less fortunate
   than we are.
6. Gifts—our tithes and offerings for the Lord and items
   for our missionary cupboard.

7. A coffee cup or pots and pans—for extending hospitality to missionaries and others of God's people as well as unsaved to whom we wish to witness.

8. A door knob—as you do visitation for the Lord.

9. Flowers—to be an encouragement and blessing to the ill and shut-ins you call upon.

10. Christian magazines—to better inform yourself and to pass on to a friend.

The list could go on and on. Don't forget that whatever you do, your hands should be yielded to the Lord and motivated by His love. Then you will see your efforts blessed and used by Him!

Speaking of hands—probably no hands are busier than a mother's hands and perhaps no tasks are more important than hers. A fitting close to this chapter would be this "jewel"—a lovely poem about her mother's hands from the pen of Eleanor Bancroft, veteran missionary and wife of Dr. Bernard Bancroft, retired chairman of the Department of World Missions at Faith Baptist Bible College. It was a blessing to me; may it be to you as well.

My picture shows you standing calm
Beside the roses fair
That always speak to me of you
Because you put them there
With hands that knew because you loved
All living beauty so,
We watched you labor o'er them
Then . . . we saw the roses grow.
My picture shows your warm brown hands,
Dear hands at rest but, oh,
Because we were demanding much
We rarely saw them so.
No picture in the world can show
What you have planted deep

Within the hearts of favored ones
God gave into your keep.
But if the world from us knows aught
That's fragrant or that's fair,
It is because with love-skilled hands
You put the beauty there!

September

December 14, 1956, was the magic date. At 8 P.M. on that snowy evening almost twenty-two years ago, Mike and I stood before our pastor in Calvary Baptist Church in Pueblo, Colorado, quietly repeated our vows, tenderly said "I will!" and "I do!" and then were pronounced by him to be husband and wife. It was a time of joy and hope, a time of old dreams come true and new dreams for the future.

One of the precious, unfulfilled dreams of that long-ago day was that, in His time, God would bless our home with children—several—the more the merrier! Years passed by and it didn't happen. We didn't understand but we did learn to say, "Thy will be done!" to our Lord. His way for us is not always what we would choose, but it is always best.

We call the college kids at Faith Baptist Bible College "our kids" and we love them. They have been a blessing in our lives. It has been fun, too, playing "Auntie and Uncle" to a host of boys and girls who are the children of dear friends and relatives.

In the summer of 1978, the Lord gave us the special privilege of having in our home for two months a real niece and nephew—Nikki, fourteen, and Erik, twelve. They are the children of my brother, Robert, who died in 1967 when they were one and three. What a change they made in the calm and quiet Doonan home!

Ladies, I have learned so many things since the last week in June that I have neither time nor space to tell them all. Besides, these are things which most of you already know.

I have a new appreciation for mothers and all that makes up their lives—the laughter, the tears, the endless drain on time and energy and emotions, the hassle of trying to make ends meet in the face of inflation and teen-age appetites, the difficulties of discipline and the thrill when progress is made. Yes, from now on I will understand the lot of mothers a bit better.

I have a new appreciation, too, for the awesome responsibility parents have to direct their children into right paths—paths that lead to spiritual life and growth. These paths are more often than not the ones the young people would detour from, and yet how vitally important they are—family and personal devotions, church attendance, Scripture memorization, right companions, wholesome activities.

The Lord gave us the unparalleled joy of seeing Nikki and Erik come to a saving knowlege of the Lord Jesus Christ while they were with us. Two beautiful, precious children this summer began the journey that will lead them at last to Heaven. We are very thankful and we covet your prayers that they may grow strong as Christians in the days ahead.

The clutter is all gone now. The kids have gone home to Colorado. No longer do I trip over a ball glove or someone's muddy sneakers as I walk through my house. No longer do I have to bake mountains of oatmeal cookies or pans and pans of pizza. In a way, I miss it—most of all, though, I miss them! And though I've prayed for them since the day they were born, my prayers now are more heartfelt, more personal, more intelligent.

God bless Nikki and Erik and girls and boys everywhere who have this summer entered "the strait gate" and now walk "the narrow way."

November

The doctors were firm in their prognosis—unless the family left the fogs of London for a more healthful climate, the one remaining son, then twenty-three, was in danger of following his two brothers in death from tuberculosis. It was a very serious situation, for the father was a noted authority in the field of speech and enjoyed a prosperous career in London teaching deaf-mutes to speak. However, it all meant little to him if his only son's life was at stake. So Melville Bell put his affairs in order and moved his family across the ocean to Brantford, Ontario, Canada, and took up his work on a new continent.

Melville Bell had earlier invented a code of symbols for use in his teaching, which he called "Visible Speech." In April 1871, young Graham, by then perfectly healthy and working in close partnership with his father, went by request from Canada to the city of Boston in the United States to teach this system to teachers of the deaf. By 1873 he was a professor at Boston University.

It was about this time that Graham began electrical experiments during his free evening hours to try to produce a "musical telegraph" which would transmit several messages at one time. So enthusiastic was he about the project that he won encouragement and financial backing from two of his deaf pupils' fathers, Gardiner Greene Hubbard, an attorney, and Thomas Sanders, a successful merchant.

As he carried on his tedious experiments, Bell began to ponder a larger idea. If other sounds could be transmitted through wires, as in the case of the telegraph, why couldn't the sound of the human voice be transmitted as well? Then, on June 2, 1875, as he worked on the line of his telegraph in one room and his assistant, Mr. Watson, worked on the reeds in another room, the sound of a plucked reed came clearly over the wire. He ran to Watson, shouting, "What did you do just then? Don't change anything!"

There followed an hour or so of experimenting with the reeds and listening to their sounds. Then the young teacher gave his assistant specifications for making the first "Bell Telephone." Alexander Graham Bell, at twenty-eight, knew his big idea was going to become a reality!

Bell received his patent on March 7, 1876, and three days later the telephone carried its first intelligible message from the attic to the basement of a rented Boston boardinghouse. Bell had spilled battery acid on his clothing and said into the instrument, "Mr. Watson, please come here! I want you!" Mr. Watson heard every word clearly and came rushing up the stairs shouting, "I can hear you! I can hear the words!" That accident was forgotten in the excitement over the success of their work.

The telephone was displayed to the public at the Centennial Exposition in Philadelphia where it attracted almost no interest—that is, until Don Pedro, the colorful young Emperor of Brazil, came by and tried it out. His eyes grew wide in amazement as he held the receiver to his ear and he cried out, "It talks! It talks!" as Mr. Bell spoke softly into the mouthpiece.

That attracted the judges, who forgot their supper

and stood around until ten o'clock that night, listening as one after another spoke into the "new-fangled machine." It was then taken from its dark display corner behind the stairs and placed in the central Judges Pavilion where passing crowds could see and marvel at this new miracle of communication.

It has been said that the telephone received the "most valuable single patent ever issued" and its invention has drastically changed the way of life for people around the world. Because of the genius and persistence of Alexander Graham Bell, today you ladies can pick up the telephones in your own homes and within a few moments of time can talk to someone almost anywhere on earth.

As great a miracle of communication and life-changing device as the telephone is, there is another greater miracle of communication far more life-changing than the telephone. It was available to man even centuries before Mr. Bell's invention. It is the miracle of prayer—that direct line to Heaven which is open day and night and which brings man into contact with Almighty God.

In less time than it takes to place a call to the next door neighbor on the telephone, the Christian can speak with his Heavenly Father to offer adoration and praise, give thanks, confess his sins, or make requests for himself and others. There is never an uncompleted call, never a busy signal, never a poor connection, never an outage because of storm and never an expensive bill to pay!

Ladies, if we would serve the Lord well we must realize that prayer is the only form of Christian service without which no other is complete, and yet prayer is a service complete in itself. If we would be effective servants of His, the sincere request of our hearts should be, as it was of the disciples, "Lord, teach us to pray" (Luke 11:1).

Speaking of telephones . . . why don't you use yours this week to invite someone to go to church with you? Then use that other miracle of communication; ask your

Father in Heaven to speak to that needy heart through what they hear in your church. May the Lord bless your outreach for Him!

★　★　★　★　★　★

It was my privilege during one day to have fellowship with two separate ladies' groups in our state. Early on that rainy morning in October, a friend and I set out on a three-hour drive to Prairie Flower Baptist Church in Washington, Iowa. It was a real treat to have time in this busy life we lead to visit as we drove, sharing one another's thoughts and joys and burdens.

We arrived at the church about 11:15 and what a beehive of activity we found! There were ladies in every room of that church basement, all working away. In addition to making curtains for all of those rooms and hanging them that day, some women were making flannelgraph backgrounds, some were preparing memory verses for Joy Clubs, and others were working on missionary projects of many kinds. This was the first of the new fall-winter all-day missionary work times they have each year. We enjoyed pitching in to help.

Following a delightful covered-dish luncheon, I shared some thoughts from God's Word. Then Marge and I were homeward-bound. I got home in time to grab a quick bite to eat, change my clothes and rush down to Grandview Park Baptist Church in Des Moines to speak to the ladies of the World-Wide Mission Group.

This was a full day but one of blessing for me as I saw you ladies busy working for the Lord, and concerned about the spread of the gospel all around the world.

Let me close our little visit together this time with this sparkling little gem of a saying which caught my imagination. I saw it on a lighted sign-board outside a church as we drove down the street one evening— "COMING SOON, IN PERSON, THE LORD JESUS CHRIST!" It is true, ladies. Keep looking up!

52

January

January, the first month of our year, was named for Janus, that character in mythology who had two faces looking in opposite directions. One face looked backward into the past and the other looked forward into the future. Janus served as the Roman god of gates and doors, entrances and exits. His name, in turn, was derived from the Latin word "janua," which means gate.

Our first month would seem to be well-named—January—the gate to the new year. And, like mythological Janus, we find ourselves standing here on New Year's Day looking in two directions—looking backward into the past year, thinking of all its joys and sorrows, blessings and trials, successes and failures, opportunities claimed and opportunities lost; at the same time looking forward into the next year with its twelve months of unspoiled, untried days and ways. We cannot help but ask, "What does this new year hold for me? How can I make this year better than any year before?"

Aren't you glad that we do not face the new year alone? Aren't you glad that when we pray, it is not to some god of myth and imagination? How blessed we are to have a personal relationship with the *living* God, the God

53

of all power, the one true God Who sent His Son to save us! We may start our year with Him. We may commit those unspoiled, untried days and ways to Him Who has promised in His Word, "I will instruct thee and teach thee in the way which thou shalt go: I will guide thee with mine eye" (Ps. 32:8).

This morning I began daily Bible readings which, if I am faithful, will take me clear through God's Word during this year. Are any of you setting this same goal?

Too often, I think, we deny (in action rather than word) the importance of time spent in quiet communion with our Lord. We bustle about, so busy in His service that we have no time for Him. May this little "gem" from my JEWEL BOX—words of wisdom from an unknown poet— be a challenge to each of us in setting priorities for the new year.

> 'Tis not the bustling hours of time
> We spend in serving Him,
> And not the deeds of service done,
> Nor yet the fame we win;
> But whether there is fellowship
> And blest communion sweet,
> For oft we may do most for Him
> By sitting at His feet.

I think, too, that we need to realize that we are who we are because God planned it that way. So many things in our lives we are helpless to change. We need to cease asking why and accept the lot God has seen fit to give us. My thanks go to my own dear mother for this anonymous poem which has a message for all of us.

> I don't know how to say it, but somehow it seems to
>   me
> That maybe we are stationed where God wants us
>   to be;

That the little place I'm filling is the reason for my
    birth
And just to do the work I do, He sent me to this
    earth.
If God had wanted otherwise, I guess He would
    have made
Me just a little different, of a worse or better grade;
And, since God knows and understands all things
    of land and sea,
i fancy that He placed me here, just where He
    wanted me.
Sometimes I get to thinking, as my labors I review,
That I should like a higher place with greater things
    to do;
But I come to the conclusion, when the envying is
    stilled,
That the post to which God sent me is the post He
    wanted filled.
So I plod along and struggle in the hope, when
    day is through,
That I'm really necessary to the things God wants to
    do;
And there isn't any service I can give which I should
    scorn,
For it may be just the reason God allowed me to be
    born.

One friend wrote to me, ". . . I was studying about the
Rapture when the thought came to me that then everyone
will be the same. That little lady in the jungles of Africa or
South America who knows the Lord may not have much
of this world's goods, but at the Rapture she will be on the
same level as some of our great preachers of today."

Isn't that a precious thought, ladies? No matter how
hard the spot in which we find ourselves here and now,
not matter how little or how much we have, a day is

coming soon when all of this will be forgotten. Together, all saints will rise to meet the Lord in the air and we shall be with Him forever!

I wonder, will that day be one of the 365 found on our brand-new calendar? It could be! May 1 John 2:28 be our watchword for this new year!

February

A poet by the name of William Leggett once considered the Bible in his hand and wrote:

> This little Book I'd rather own than all the
>   gold and gems
> That e'er in monarchs coffers shone,
>   than all their diadems.
> Nay, were the seas one chrysolite,
>   the earth a golden ball,
> And diamonds all the stars of night,
>   this Book were worth them all!

My own heart echoes a hearty "Amen!" to his sentiments. What a treasure we have in God's written Word! How apropos to every situation of our lives are the words we read upon its pages!

During the past month, I was reminded again of a very familiar but very special portion of Scripture and it was a help to me on one particular day.

It was one of those bright, frigid mornings with the wind chill way down below zero. I bustled about getting ready for work, all the time dreading to go out.

Finally, Mike and I sat down at our new, round, maple

table for breakfast and devotions before going our separate ways to meet the day. As Mike prayed that morning, he asked the Lord to grant me safety as I drove on the icy streets and then said something to the effect that he knew the Lord had a plan for our day; might we accept and fulfill it.

A few moments later I was driving between mountains of blue-shadowed snow the five blocks to the IARBC (Iowa Association of Regular Baptist Churches) state office where I serve as Mr. Brong's secretary. I turned carefully into the parking lot, glad the Lord had brought me there safely as Mike had prayed.

Just then, a big, blue pick-up truck backed from a parking place in front of the dentist's office a couple of doors down and rammed hard into my left-front fender. It happened so quickly I didn't have time to honk my horn, or even get scared.

The poor man who hit me was so elated at just finishing a series of eight dental appointments that he backed out without even looking to see if anyone was behind him. He found out there was!

As I stood looking at the crumpled fender of our "new" used car—a $650 crumple on the car we wouldn't even begin payments on for two more weeks—I said to my boss who had just driven in, "I don't want to tell Mike!"

But I did. I called him on the phone and he took the news as a Christian husband should—was glad no one was hurt—then reminded me that we had prayed about God's plan for our day. Since this had happened, it was evidently part of God's plan for me.

Like a spoiled child, I thought to myself, *but I don't understand why!* And, quick as a flash, this message from God's Word came into my mind: "And we know that all things work together for good to them that love God, to them who are the called according to his purpose" (Rom. 8:28).

All things! I might not know *why,* but I could know that this unpleasant experience would work together with the other things God had planned for my day for my good.

I was rather shaken and trembly for a while because nothing like that had ever happened to me before, but the verse helped me again as it had helped me many times before. Just before leaving the office for lunch, I turned to my typewriter and put down these words:

> I do not always understand
> All things that God for me has planned—
> The things that seem to mar my day,
> The trials that fall across my way—
> And yet, because I love the Lord,
> I trust the promise of His Word
> That "all things" (though some may seem ill)
> Shall work together, in His will,
> For my own good. Thus, in God's hand
> I'll leave what I don't understand.

March

These words are being written to you on a Sunday afternoon. Dinner is done, the dishes are put away and I cherish these few quiet moments at my desk. The north wind that is whistling around the corners of my house and the snow blowing against the windowpane bring no chill at all to the spiritual warmth of the Lord's Day.

Sunday is such a special day for the Christian—what the hymnwriter called, "Day of all the week the best!" Not only is it symbolic of the resurrection of our Lord on the first day of the week, but it is that day when strength is renewed as we rest in the Lord, encouragement is received as we fellowship with His people and direction and guidance for our everyday living come from the rich ministry of His Word.

Each Sunday morning it is my privilege to be a part of a women's class taught by Ann Davison, the wife of our pastor. Right now we are going through the book of Proverbs together and learning, oh, so many things the Lord wants us to know.

As this godly woman teaches our class, we who are her students and who love and respect her are learning far more than just words from the Word of God. We are learning through her example how to put the words into practice. Anecdotes, examples, prayer requests she shares with us—all give glimpses into a life where practical application is made of the truth she seeks to teach.

Often I find myself breathing a prayer from my heart—"Lord, thank you for my pastor's wife!" And then I realize that there are scores like her all across the country. Have you thanked the Lord lately for your pastor's wife?

You know, being a pastor's wife has to be one of the most difficult callings a woman can have. Read this poem by an unknown poet and try to realize some of the difficulties which are faced every day by that sweet lady in your parsonage.

> You may think it quite an easy task
> Or just a pleasant life,
> But really, it takes a lot of grace
> To be a pastor's wife!
> She's supposed to be a paragon
> Without a fault in view,
> A "saint" when in the parsonage
> As well as in the pew.
> Her home must be a small hotel
> For folks who chance to roam,
> And yet have peace and harmony—
> The "perfect" preacher's home.
> Whenever groups are called to meet,
> Her presence must be there;
> And yet the members all agree
> She should live a life of prayer.
> Though hearing people's burdens
> And griefs both night and day,
> She's supposed to spread but sunshine
> To all along the way.
> She must lend a sympathetic ear
> To every tale of woe

And then forget about it
Lest it to others go.
Her children must be models
Of sweetness and of poise,
But still stay on the level
Of other girls and boys.
Yes, you may think it easy
Or just a pleasant life,
But really, it takes a lot of grace
To be a pastor's wife!

Ladies, I challenge you as I challenge myself—let's pray for her and be more understanding and appreciative of the pastor's wife in the days ahead.

And if you want to do something extra-special to let her know you love and appreciate her, here are a couple of ideas that came my way—

1. How about a "Dollar Shower" for her? This would be on no special holiday or birthday, but on an ordinary day and done out of love and appreciation. Have all the ladies of your church send a friendship card with a dollar bill tucked inside on the same day. Instruct her that the dollars are to be used for something special just for her—not for bills, not for the kids, not for her husband—just for her! What a blessing and encouragement such a shower of love could be!

2. Celebrate her birthday by taking a "surprise party" to her house. Check with the pastor to be sure she will be home. Bring simple refreshments along and make the gift items from each one something to help with all the entertaining she does—candles, paper napkins, paper plates and cups, even baked goods she can put in her freezer for emergencies.

There are many things you can do as an individual, too, to be a blessing in the life of your pastor's wife. May the Lord use you! This can be a ministry, too!

And now, to close off for this time, a "jewel" of a recipe from the kitchen of a busy pastor's wife in Michigan. Her "Six-Week Muffins" are yummy!

SIX-WEEK MUFFINS

Pour 1 cup boiling water over 2 Shredded Wheat biscuits. Add 1 cup raisins. Cool a little, then add 1 stick soft oleo. Cool a little more, then add 1½ cups sugar, 2 eggs, 1 teaspoon salt, 2 teaspoons soda, 2½ cups flour, 2 cups All-Bran cereal, 2 cups buttermilk. Mix well. Store covered in the refrigerator up to six weeks. Spoon into muffin tins when needed, without stirring. Bake at 425 degrees for 15-20 minutes. Delicious!

April

With the coming of the month of April, many things come to cheer the hearts of winter-weary souls . . . the greening of the grass; the beauty of crocuses and hyacinths, tulips and jonquils; the sound of birdsong in the air; balmy spring breezes to dry those clothes hanging outside on the line once again; the joy of digging in the moist earth and planting tiny seeds which will soon display the "resurrection power" the Lord has placed within them. At least, this is what April is *supposed* to bring to Iowa. But, wouldn't you know it, as I look from my window this morning, it is snowing again! I can't believe it!

Yesterday was a beautiful day. The calendar said April 3, and I was up early. By 7:30 I was driving north on I-35, praising the Lord for good weather and the opportunity of attending the N.E. Area Regional Ladies' Meeting. I picked up our state chairman, Lorraine Strohbehn, and by 9:00 we were at the bottom of the hill in downtown Union, Iowa, where a marker right in the middle of the intersection pointed toward Calvary Baptist Church.

What a treat to be motioned right up to the front steps, where one of the church men offered to park our car so we wouldn't get muddy feet! I'm sure all of the ladies who came were thankful for this special service.

The pastor's wife and her ladies had done a tremendous job of planning and preparing a very special day around the theme, FOOTPRINTS OF JESUS. Of course, our name tags were in the shape of footprints (pink ones!) and after registration everyone enjoyed coffee and cookies.

FBHM missionaries Robert and Kathy Gough were also a great blessing as they sang and spoke during the day. Though physically blind, this couple has great spiritual insight and were a challenge to all of us.

After a delicious luncheon which included homemade cupcakes for dessert, three workshops were offered. Robert Gough presented "Walking with Him on the Job," Kathy Gough spoke about "Walking with Your Mate," and I shared some thoughts with a large group of mothers and grandmothers based on the teaching of God's Word concerning "Walking As Parental Examples." Also, it was a blessing for me to speak to the entire group about walking with the Lord at our closing session.

Now, some of the ladies asked for an outline and some poetry from the workshop. Here they are!

I. Be a good example to help your child in his relationship to God.
   A. Be saved—this is most important of all. You should be able to lead your child to Christ!
   B. Be steadfast—live a consistent Christian life seven days a week *(1 Pet. 2:21; 1 Tim. 4:12)*!
   C. Be spiritually minded—personal and family devotions, prayer, church attendance and your everyday life are a measure of this!
   D. Be submissive—this area includes being submissive to God's will, to God's Word and to your husband!

II. Be a good example to help your child in his relationship to himself.
   A. Teach the value of life *(Gen. 2:7; Acts 17:25)*.
   B. Teach the value of time *(Eph. 5:15–17)*.
   C. Teach the value of work *(Ps. 90:17)*.
   D. Teach the value of play *(Col. 3:23)*.
   E. Teach the value of purity *(Ps. 19:14; Phil. 4:8)*.
   F. Teach the value of cleanliness and good grooming *(1 Tim. 4:12)*.

III. Be a good example to help your child in his relationship to others.
   A. Be loving and affectionate.
   B. Be friendly and hospitable.
   C. Be generous and unselfish.
   D. Be kind and understanding.
   E. Be fair and considerate.
   F. Be trustworthy and honest.
   G. Be respectful and submissive.
   H. Be courteous and mannerly.

And here is the poem from an unknown author:

Mary had a little boy, his life was
    white as snow;
He never went to Sunday School
    'cause Mary wouldn't go.
He never heard the tales of Christ
    that thrill a childish mind;
While other children went to class,
    this child was left behind.
And so he grew from babe to youth
    —she saw to her dismay
A life that once was snowy white
    become a dingy gray.
Realizing he was lost,
    she tried to win him back,

But soon the life that once was white
    had turned an ugly black!
She even started back to church,
    and Bible study, too;
She begged the preacher, "Isn't there
    a thing that you can do?"
The preacher tried and failed and said,
    "We're just too far behind!
I tried to tell you years ago, but
    you would pay no mind."
And so, another child is lost whose life
    was white as snow,
Sunday School could have helped
    —but Mary wouldn't go.

One lady I spoke with at the meeting told me of
something their group was trying for the first time this
year and I thought some of you might appreciate the idea.
In order to keep the missionary cupboard well stocked at
their church, each lady is asked to give the cupboard a
"birthday present" when her birthday rolls around.

Speaking of birthdays, I was born in the tiny
mountain town of Reserve, New Mexico, on April 16, in
the depression year of 1934. I have always wished I could
find a "birthday twin." Could there be one for me among
some of you?

May

On a white, lace doily in the center of my round, maple dining table is something new. I wish you could see how pretty it looks in the bright May sunshine that floods through my kitchen window. It is a birthday gift from very dear friends—a lovely, fluffy candle ring of silk flowers that look so real I find myself hoping they won't wilt. Morning glories! Their clear, heavenly blue sets off to perfection the darker blue candle they surround

Morning glories have always been one of my favorite flowers. Looking at them here on my table brings back many memories of long ago days when I was a child—when life moved at a considerably slower pace and seemed not so complicated as it often does now.

I remember crystal-clear Colorado mornings—the hum of bees over the old-fashioned garden of the little old lady who lived next door—grass sparkling with diamond dew-drops—blue morning glories blooming on a fence. Morning glory time always seemed to me one of the best parts of the day!

Now that I have grown older, and especially since I have grown older in the Lord, "Morning Glory Time" still seems to me one of the best parts of the day. Pardon the play on words. I'm sure you know what I mean.

Every Christian should have a "Morning Glory Time" to start the day—a time in the early hours of freshness to meet with the Lord, worship at His feet, talk to Him in prayer, receive strength and guidance for the coming hours from His Word and lift the heart in praise that the mercies of our God are "new every morning." Our very souls are filled with "Morning Glory" as we ponder His great faithfulness (Lam. 3:22, 23)!

I read a poem just recently by a lady named Laura Snow which seems to be a perfect prayer for the "Morning Glory Time" of the Christian homemaker. I share it in the hope that it may be a blessing to you today.

> Amid the duties of today,
> In all I think and do and say,
> Whether I work, or rest, or play—
> Lord, keep me sweet at home.
> When household duties claim my care
> And I seem needed everywhere,
> Then turn my heart to praise and prayer,
> And keep me sweet at home.
> No matter what the day may bring,
> Or night; I pray in everything
> My life may glorify my King—
> Especially at home!

June

At just about one o'clock in the morning on Thursday, May 31st, our little car came over the crest of a hill on the highway into Ankeny and we saw, twinkling out to us through the night like a myriad of diamonds, THE LIGHTS OF HOME!

The annual week in Colorado had been wonderful—visiting with loved ones till all hours—marvelling over how much the nieces and nephews had grown—renewing old friendships and making some new ones—enjoying that special bond of fellowship with brothers and sisters in Christ which we find wherever we go. As we drove along familiar streets and felt the bright warmth of that Rocky Mountain sunshine, our minds seemed to whirl in a kaleidoscope of happy memories, for Pueblo was the town where we grew up, and learned to love one another, and began our life together. I wonder how many times that week we caught ourselves turning to one another to ask, "Do you remember. . . ?"

Yes, the week was wonderful—but, oh, THE LIGHTS OF HOME! No matter how wonderful a time we have

70

anywhere else, it seems like coming home is the very best part of all. Do you feel that way, too?

Mike's mother came back to Iowa with us, and a couple of days later we drove her down to her childhood home near Deep River for a visit with relatives, and a special reunion and birthday celebration.

Happy reunions and the lights of home have served to remind me again that one day every one of us who belongs to God's family will be "at Home" with Him! That will be a reunion which will never end, in a place of unbelievable beauty. And the "Light" of that "Home" will never dim—God's Word says that our Savior, the Lord Jesus Christ, "the Lamb is the light thereof" (Rev. 21:23).

Among the letters waiting for me when I returned from vacation was a very welcome one from Perry, Iowa, supplying the following recipe. I promise you, it is worth trying.

THREE-LAYER NO-BAKE COOKIES

First Layer:
Place in the top of a double boiler and cook until blended:
 ½ cup butter; ¼ cup sugar; ¼ cup cocoa; 1 teaspoon
 vanilla.
Add: 1 egg, lightly beaten. Cook 5 minutes longer, stirring.
Add: 2 cups graham cracker crumbs, finely crushed; 1 cup
 flaked coconut; ½ cup chopped nuts.
Press mixture into a 9″ x 13″ pan. Cool.
Second Layer:
Cream until light and fluffy: ½ cup butter.
Mix and add to butter: 3 tablespoons milk; 1 full package
 instant vanilla pudding mix; 2 cups confectioner's sugar.
 Add gradually and beat untill smooth. Spread over first
 layer and let stand until firm.
Third Layer:
Melt in a double boiler: 1 six-ounce package real chocolate
 chips; 1½ tablespoons butter; 2 tablespoons milk. Spread
 over second layer. Cut into squares or small bars before
 chocolate becomes completely hardened. Store in the
 refrigerator.

 # August

A dear friend had invited me over for lunch and it was in her kitchen that it happened. We were at the table, enjoying the fellowship and lingering over a final cup of tea when the long necklace I was wearing (my favorite!) got caught on the sharp edge of the table, snapping the string and sending tiny, shiny red beads in every direction. Oh, dear! I hope I found them all and didn't miss any!

My thoughts on this hot July afternoon are like the broken string of beads—going in every direction. I hope I don't miss anything I want to share with you today.

First of all, a few ideas for your file. They may come in handy sometime.

NUT-CUPS—I wonder how many of you have discovered how beautifully the "foam" egg cartons can be turned into nut-cups for your special event. They come in a variety of pretty pastel colors and can be trimmed to fit your theme with a bit of lace, a few pipe-cleaners, a few sheets of construction paper.

Why not have your ladies start saving them now? As they come in, cut away all but the little egg sections and when banquet-time rolls around again, you will be one jump ahead.

Oh, yes! If your banquet happens to be a missionary one, a clever nut-cup idea is to make tiny "native huts." Use the conventional paper nut-cups you buy in a brown color and cover with a "thatched roof." Easy to make! Cut a circle of construction paper a bit larger than your cup, slit on one side to the center, slip one edge of the cut over the other just slightly and glue in place. Cover the top of the little cone with glue and put in place little pieces of straw. Then, watch for the smiles when your banquet guests find out the "roofs" come off and there are goodies inside!

Missionary Cupboard—I heard of one ladies' group in our fellowship that always has a full cupboard. Their secret? They "shower" it at every monthly meeting! Their project chairman is in charge of this and informs the ladies ahead of each meeting of the type of items they should bring that month. One time it will be toilet articles; another, linens; later, men's items or things especially for the MKs. I think this is terrific!

And how about this?—At vacationtime I learned of a ladies group (not of our denomination) that has an **historian** for their group. She is an elected officer and it is her job to make a scrapbook for the year featuring all meetings and special events of the group. She doesn't just write it up—she takes pictures to include. This makes a wonderful and interesting record of what the ladies have done—a real treasure for some future church anniversary!

"Mother-Daughter Season" has come and gone again, and I rejoiced in the privilege to share this happy time with many ladies throughout the state this year.

After all my own speaking was done, I was invited to go along with a friend to Winterset, Iowa, one evening while she did the honors. This was a real treat and the theme of "Flowers" was lovely.

To begin with, each person who came through the

door received a beautiful "corsage" from a basket of
tissue flowers someone had spent lots of time making.

The friend who spoke at the banquet will be leaving
to go to Japan for one year as a short-term teacher of
missionary children under ABWE. She shared this burden
with the ladies, but also included in her talk something
about mothers and grandmothers which I asked if I might
share with you. I think it will be a blessing to you as it was
to me.

MOTHERS

A mother is someone dear to the heart,
Who's known you and loved you
   right from the start.
She multiplies faith when problems
   are tough,
And divides up her love so each child
   has enough.
A mother reads stories of dragons and kings;
She can build a great castle with
   boxes and things.
She teaches her children the alphabet
From a round oatmeal box or a
   word-scramble set.
A mother is special to girls and to fellows;
She knows the right time to carry umbrellas.
She teaches good manners, sews a fine
   seam,
Understands life, and believes in your dream.
A mother is memories through
   rose-colored glass.
She's warm apple pie; a lady with class.
Her children go forth insured with her prayers
And a truth universal—it's mother who cares!

That poem was written by a woman by the name of

Alice Mason while this description of "What A
Grandmother Is" comes from a fourth-grade student in
Augusta, Georgia.

"A grandmother is a lady who has no little children
of her own, so she likes other people's folks. A
grandfather is a man grandmother. He goes for
walks with boys and they talk about fishing and
cars and like that. Grandmas don't have to do
anything except be there. They are older so they
shouldn't play hard or run. It is enough if they
drive us to the store where the pretend horse is
and have lots of dimes ready. Or if they take us for
walks, they slow down past things like pretty leaves
and caterpillars. They never say 'hurry up.' Usually
they are fat, but not too fat to tie a kid's shoes.
Some wear glasses and they can take their teeth
and gums off. It's better if they don't typewrite
except with us. They don't have to be smart, only
answer questions like why dogs chase cats, or how
come God isn't married. They don't talk baby-talk
like visitors do, because it's hard to understand.
When they read to us they don't skip words or
mind if it is the same story again. Everybody
should try to have one, especially if you don't have
television, because grandmas are the only
grown-ups who have got time."

September

One cold day last March, when the snow still lay white on the land and the winter winds had not yet deserted Iowa, Mike and I went to a garden center in Des Moines. There, surrounded by gardening implements of every kind, brightly colored seed packets, bags of lawn fertilizer and weed killer, and even some forced tulips and hyacinths in clay pots, one could feel that spring really was just around the corner and it was time to think of outdoor work.

We didn't buy much that day, but before we left I picked up one small envelope of seeds and gave the clerk forty-five cents in exchange. I smiled at my husband and shrugged my shoulders and I knew he understood why. We were both thinking of our lack of success last year with that particular vegetable.

In time the snow vanished under the rays of springtime's sun, the winter winds whistled off to some other clime, and the day came when the little envelope was torn open. The seeds were dropped into the warm, brown earth and it was patted into smooth, rounded hills. Then we waited, a bit skeptically, to see what would happen.

Most of you have probably already guessed the end of the story, and know as well as I do that this was a good year for zucchini squash in Iowa! Our seeds sprouted and in June our harvest began. Those first two fruits, picked when tiny and tender and diced into a green salad, gave no token of the size our crop would eventually become.

You know how it is, don't you? When zucchini gets to bearing, picking is an everyday process. You wonder where they all come from and when they have had time to grow. And, if you happen to miss a hidden one for a few days—well, I really don't like them as well after they get to be more than a foot long!

All through the summer we enjoyed zucchini at least one meal almost every day. I browned it in butter, baked it, made it into a squash and sausage casserole, simmered it barely tender in spaghetti sauce, melted cheese over it, served it raw (sliced thin and salted) as an appetizer, dried it into snacking chips and for use during the coming winter months, etc., etc. In a catalog which came to our home, a book was advertised which contained only zucchini recipes. I wondered if I should order it!

The days my husband liked best were those when the house was filled with the spicy fragrance that told him I was baking zucchini nut bread for the freezer. He just loves it! And yesterday, Labor Day, I used up the end of our zucchini crop by baking a double batch.

As I thought about this bounty from our backyard garden, and the unbelievable way the zucchini produced this year, I said to myself, "Wouldn't it be wonderful, Gladys Doonan, if the fruit of the Spirit was produced in your life in the same abundant manner as those few hills of squash produced their fruit?!"

The fruit of the Spirit—it is enumerated for us in Galatians 5:22, 23: ". . . love, joy, peace, longsuffering, gentleness, goodness, faith, meekness, temperance. . . ." What precious fruit! Fruit that should have a place and effect in the life of every Christian woman.

What changes might it make for us and our loved ones were it borne abundantly! Too often, with myself at least, I'm afraid there is a "crop failure" or a very sparse bearing at any rate.

I wonder if the Lord, that Great Husbandman, doesn't often look down at me and shake His head as I shook my head over the zucchini plants of the year before.

With the coming of autumn, the growing season in Iowa is coming to a close for another year. However, for the Christian, there is never an end to the "growing season." Let us pray for one another and may God grant that in our personal lives, in our homes, in our communities, and in our churches in days to come we may, as women of His, grow, and flourish, and bear an abundant harvest of the fruit of the Spirit, to the glory of our Lord!

October

Several weeks ago when I went into church on Sunday morning, I was, as usual, handed a bulletin by one of our "greeters." If you know me at all, you know the first thing I do with a bulletin is turn it over to read the poem on the back. That particular morning, the poem was a "jewel," so I thought it should go into the "jewel box." It is by Margaret K. Frazer, entitled "God's Extras," and goes like this.

God could have made the sun to rise
    Without such splendor in the skies;
He could have made the sun to set
    Without a glory greater yet.

He could have made the corn to grow
    Without that sunny, golden glow;
The fruit without those colors bright,
    So pleasant to the taste and sight.

And caused the apple trees to bloom
    Without the scent that doth perfume
Those dainty blossoms, pink and white,
    That fill our hearts with sheer delight.

He could have made the ocean roll
    Without such music for the soul—
The mighty anthem, loud and strong—
    And birds without their clear, sweet song.

The charm of kitten's dainty grace,
    The dimples in a baby's face—
All these are "extras" from His hand,
    Whose love we cannot understand.

The God Who fashioned flow'rs and trees,
    Delights to give us things that please,
And all His handiwork so fair
    His glory and His love declare.

Yes, He Who made the earth and skies
    Gave "extras" for our ears and eyes,
And while my heart with rapture sings,
    I thank Him for the "extra things."

I read that poem several times during the day and it was a blessing to me. I began thinking about "God's extras" and I realized that He not only gives us "extras" in the beauties of His creation, but in a spiritual sense as well. Let me tell you what I mean.

The moment we believe in Christ as personal Savior, we receive the wonderful gift of salvation—forgiveness of sin and eternal life. But that is not all! There are many, many "extras" that come from a loving Father to His own children. Immediately, of course, there is the peace that comes from a right relationship with God. There is the indwelling Holy Spirit Who is our Comforter, our Guide, our Teacher.

And what about the blessing of having God's own Holy Word, the Bible? He could have chosen another means of sending His message to man, but isn't it wonderful that He gave it to us in His Word—His Word that we can have to read over and over again, to study, to memorize, to help us through all of life!

Another "extra," and a precious one it is, is the joy of Christian fellowship. There is nothing like the special bond of love between those who know the Lord. Wherever we go, we find this with other believers, even when we have never met them before. What a blessing to have Christian friends—those best friends we laugh and cry with, pray with and grow with!

There is the privilege of serving the Lord. That, too, is an "extra" given to us through His grace. To have a part in the ministry of the gospel by going, by giving, by praying, by encouraging, by helping in practical ways—we should not take this lightly.

More extras? There is the difference the Lord makes in our homes—there is the assurance that He is in control of our lives and our world—there is the strength He provides when trials come—there is the blessed hope we have for the future. And on, and on, and on! All "extras" given to us by our God. What thankful people we should be! Let's try to remember to thank Him every day from now on for all the "extras" He sends into our lives.

November

"Absent from the body . . . present with the Lord!"
What a comfort and blessing these words are to us when
our hearts ache because of the passing of one whom we
love. For that one, we know it is "far better." Yet, we who
are left behind do sorrow, though "not as those who have
no hope." Our confidence is that God knows best, that He
is too good to be unkind and too wise to make mistakes!

During this past week we have had cause to think
about these truths once again. God, in His goodness and
wisdom, chose to take one of the brightest of His "little
jewels" to Himself. His name was Paul Andrew Sammons.
He was two and a half years old. He was the son of Gary
and Wilma and the little brother of Beth Ann and Jimmy.
And, being "absent from the body," we know he is
"present with the Lord."

Gary and Wilma Sammons have been special to us
for a long time. Wilma came to Omaha Baptist Bible
College for her first year the same year my husband
joined the music faculty. He sang for her wedding in Des
Moines after graduation, and we were glad for the
dedication of this young couple to the Lord's will.

We exchanged letters during the time they spent in Dallas at seminary. We rejoiced with them when Beth Ann was born. We prayed for them as they spent a year in Mexico at language school.

Then, "confronting Chile's challenge," they left for South America under ABWE and they were in a special sense "our missionaries." Jimmy joined the family and he found his place in our hearts, too, even before we ever saw him.

In the fall of 1976, we were thrilled to receive word that a new baby was expected in the springtime. When word came of his safe arrival, I wrote an acrostic birth announcement on his name as I had done for the other two children and sent it off to the printer.

We could hardly wait for the Sammons to arrive home from the field so we could see this new member of their family. And from the day we first saw little Paul in the Des Moines airport, we knew that he was a very special little boy.

Gary was invited to join the faculty of FBBC to head up the missions program and something we had never expected happened—the Sammons became our "neighbors" as they purchased a home only three blocks from ours.

So, for a couple of years it was our delight to watch little Paul grow. We saw him learn to walk—we heard him learn to talk, and laughed over the funny things he said. We felt a lump in our throats when we first heard him sing "Jesus Loves Me" in our car one evening after prayer meeting.

And our hearts were broken with those of our dear friends when we received word that a tragic drowning had taken that little life.

Charles Bergerson of Faith Baptist Bible College wrote a poem for Paul's parents—perhaps it will be a blessing to you.

Little Paul wrote no epistle
But the smile upon his face;
Little Paul fulfilled no mission
But to charm a world with grace.

Little Paul fathered no churches,
Yet he blessed the sainted throng
With his "Jesus Loves Me" message
From the pulpit of his song!

Little Paul was no apostle,
Yet for two and one-half years
He sustained a faithful witness
In this vale of human tears.

Little Paul before no rulers
Stood, as once his namesake did;
Yet no ruler is so wise who
In Paul's Saviour is not hid.

But, behold how Jesus loved this
Little Paul of Sammons' home,
Who in months fulfilled God's purpose
Lest on earth he useless roam.

Little Paul served God in shortness,
As the greater Paul in length;
Yet their crowns will be quite equal.
As their days, so was their strength.

Whom the Lord Himself hath given,
He hath taken to Himself.
Blessed be the name, Jehovah,
Our Sustainer, Friend and Help.

    Because of Little Paul's death, we have thought more
about Heaven during recent days. We have been
reminded of its glories described for us in God's
Word—the beauty of jasper walls and gates of pearl and

streets of gold; the freedom there from sin and death and sorrow; the assurance that God will there wipe away all our tears, once and for all; and above everything, the presence of our dear Savior Who is Himself the Light of that place.

As the Thanksgiving season comes this year, I am thankful for the hope of Heaven. I am thankful that little Paul, with his unforgettable smile and sparkling eyes, is there safe and happy with Jesus. I am thankful that one day we who love him and know Christ will see him again, as well as other loved ones who have known the Lord and have gone before. I am thankful, too, for all who have helped to uphold the Sammons in prayer and fellowship at this time of sadness.

May the Lord bless you this Thanksgiving with a truly thankful heart and much for which to be thankful!

January

On a long ago Christmas, more years back than I like to remember, one of the gaily wrapped packages which bore my name and which I had the fun of opening contained a very special toy. Its name, which I could not then even pronounce, was a kaleidoscope.

I loved it! I could dream all kinds of dreams as I sat with my eye to the tiny peep-hole in the top of the cylinder. Slowly, slowly I would turn it around and, inside, little bits of colored glass would change their positions, making jewel-like reflections forming all sorts of fascinating and beautiful patterns.

Often I would stop and call to Mother or Daddy or one of my brothers to "come see this one!" But, alas! Changing the little instrument from hand to hand would change the pattern, too, and the beautiful sight which caused me to exclaim was gone forever.

Several years ago, on another Christmas, a special friend of mine—one who knows all my secrets and thus knows I have never outgrown my love for kaleidoscopes—gave me another kaleidoscope.

It is a new kind, very sophisticated, designed for

adults, I think. There are not bits of colored glass inside, only mirrors. You still look into a tiny hole at the top while you turn the tube slowly around. You still see beautiful patterns, but these patterns are made by whatever you point the instrument toward, for the bottom is covered by glass. Dishes, furniture, fireplace bricks, pets, people's faces—all become beautiful and fascinating patterns when they come within the aim of this kaleidoscope.

It is January, and as we stand at the threshold of a new year we have been changing calendars at our house. I suppose you have, too. Just now as I sat flipping through the pages of the little engagement calendar which fits into my purse, a pencilled line here and there turned the year just past into a kaleidoscope for me. Memories came flashing through my mind in bits and pieces, forming jewel-like patterns lovely to behold, making me want to share with someone else.

Every imaginable color and tint and hue is there. Predominating, perhaps, are the warm tones of love and friendship, fellowship and sharing, happiness and harmony at home. But there were weddings and funerals, joy and sorrow, adding the contrasting shades of light and dark.

There were places to go—meetings, recitals, banquets, reunions, parties, concerts, celebrations—a rainbow whirl of "busyness."

There were tasks to do—some of them heavy, some of them light; some of them difficult, some of them simple; all of them necessary for our growth and profit in character. Each task added its own special color to the year now gone. There were precious quiet hours spent with the Word of God and in prayer—these added a rosy glow as they brought spiritual health.

And through the kaleidoscopic colors of every pattern of the past year, shining with the deep, rich glint of pure gold, was the love of God—His love manifested in the provision of our every need, spiritual and material; His love manifested in the revelation of His will day by day; His love manifested in blessings of every kind, too numerous to mention here!

At this season, I think all of us are wondering what the new year will hold. Should the Lord tarry, in just twelve swiftly flying months this year, too, will be just a kaleidoscope of colored memories.

To some extent, at least, the patterns our personal lives take in this new year will depend upon ourselves. As with my newer kaleidoscope, those patterns will depend upon where we set our aims. High or low, the choice is up to us. Every day we should "look up" and determine to honor the Lord no matter what we find on our schedules.

I have chosen as my special verse for this new year Psalm 143:10. It is the prayer of my heart to the Lord. "Teach me to do thy will; for thou art my God: thy spirit is good; lead me into the land of uprightness."

Happy New Year, ladies! May each coming day form a pattern of loveliness for you.

February

For a long time I had been aware that something was wrong. The keen response to spiritual things was fading, and the warm fellowship in the Lord we once enjoyed was becoming non-existent. I wanted to help, but I didn't know the problem.

Then she said it—this woman whose witness for the Lord had once been a challenge to me. She said it with a rebellious gleam in her eye and a rebellious note in her voice. "I'm tired of being trapped at home, always doing for others, never having any time for myself. From now on I'm going to be my own woman—do my own thing!"

"Be my own woman—do my own thing!" Those newly popular phrases grated harshly on my ears, coming as they did from Christian lips. The philosophy of the day, a worldly philosophy, the ERA philosophy, had reached into a Christian home, bred discontent in a Christian wife and mother, and snatched away all the happiness once there.

Heartache followed in the wake of her decision and, though years have passed, it is not all over yet. I was quite far down on the list of those she hurt, but there was

heartache in me, too, as I watched the consequences—
heartache enough that I lay sleepless many nights,
thinking, praying, puzzling over the situation, seeking
answers.

I found those answers, too. They were right there in
God's Word where the answers to all of life's problems are
found.

To **"be my own woman"**—this is directly opposed to
the teaching of the Bible. The Christian is told very plainly,
"Ye are not your own" (1 Cor. 6:19). We have been
"bought with a price." We should be saying instead,
"From now on I'm going to be **God's woman!**" and then
totally yield ourselves to His will, whatever that is for us.
Submission, not rebellion, should be the evidence of our
strength!

To "**do my own thing**"—this is wrong, too. The Lord
Jesus Christ, Who set the perfect example for us, lived a
totally selfless life. His thought was ALWAYS for
others—even in His death. Read again Philippians 2 and
note especially those third and fourth verses. Then go on
and consider our Lord's humility and the price with which
we are bought. What would be our case today if He had
thought only of self?

The Christian woman does have a responsibility to
develop and use the talents and abilities God has given to
her—BUT only within the bounds of His will and only as
she can do it without hurting others. She must set
priorities. She must be faithful and content—AND
HAPPY—where God has placed her.

God tells us more than once in His Word that we
should not be "weary in well doing" (Gal. 6:9; 2 Thess.
3:13). And faithfully doing the tasks which are ours to
do—even if it is *only* caring for home and family—is
"well doing."

We should never forget for a moment the influence
our actions have upon others—how much others can be

hurt when we act selfishly. Apart from pleasing God, which should be our first priority in life, we must remember our families, our friends, our church, unsaved neighbors and acquaintances and those to whom we have born witness. How will our actions affect their lives?

Many years ago, when I was only in junior high school, I heard a beautiful hymn sung as a solo by one of my friends. Though it is not often used anymore, I have never forgotten it. Its words are a good reminder of our influence and responsibility. Perhaps we would do well to sing it once in a while. Some of those words go like this—

> I would be true, for there are those who trust me;
> I would be pure, for there are those who care.
> I would be strong, for there is much to suffer;
> I would be brave, for there is much to dare.
>
> I would be prayerful thru each busy moment;
> I would be constantly in touch with God;
> I would be tuned to hear His slightest whisper;
> I would have faith to keep the path Christ trod.

This is my desire, for me. I hope it is yours, for you!

March

Do you like to read? I do! I learned how quite early, because on that warm, autumn day that I entered first grade in Albuquerque, New Mexico, I was only five years old. My teacher was Miss Montoya—and I loved her! I loved school! And very few days passed by until I found that I loved books! Ever since that time, reading has been my number one, tip-top, favorite pastime.

I can remember my folks asking what I wanted for Christmas and, year after year, books were very near the top of my list. I can remember, too, their consternation that holiday of my fourth-grade year, when the stack of about a dozen books I was given for Christmas was completed by New Year's day, and I begged for more.

When I neglected to do my little chores around home, my mother would blame the books and say in exasperation, "If the house was burning down, I think you would sit in a chair and read a book!"

In the sad days following my father's death when I was eleven, there were books which helped to ease the hurt and help me forget for a few minutes our loss. Mother read aloud to my brothers and me the "Sugar

Creek Gang" books by Paul Hutchens. I wonder if she
knows how much those hours meant to me at the time,
and how they have been a treasured memory down
through the years. A while later I discovered Grace
Livingston Hill, and to this day I thank the Lord for her
Christian novels that planted healthy values and high
ideals in at least one teen-aged girl.

Of course, as I grew older I learned that priorities had
to be set in life. No matter how much fun it is to read,
sometimes a book must be laid aside for something more
important. Nevertheless, not too many things make me
happier today than having the leisure to curl up in a
corner somewhere with a good book.

The very sight of my bookshelves at home, filled to
overflowing with volumes by my favorite authors, is very
satisfying. Porter, Aldrich, Montgomery, Turnbull,
Hutchens, Arnold—they are all there and they are good
friends. However, it seems no matter how full the shelves
become, there is always one more book I want so I haunt
bookstores and used-book sales.

Fiction, non-fiction, biography, history, poetry,
inspiration, reference—fat volumes, thin volumes, tall
volumes or small—they are in bindings of every color and
quality, leather to paperback. They are my beloved books.

BUT (and you note the capital letters, I hope!), there
is one Book I own that is of more value, of more
information, inspiration, counsel and comfort than any
other on my full shelves. I purpose to read from it every
day, and as I carry out that purpose I always find
something new, fresh and exciting. It is the BOOK OF
BOOKS, God's Word, the Bible—that Book which is settled
forever in Heaven (Ps. 119:89); that which God has exalted
even above His Name (Ps. 138:2). Thank God for this
Book—His Book! When He gives it such a high place,
surely He expects us to do the same.

D. L. Moody was a great servant of the Lord, a man

who loved God's Word. The following words were copies from the flyleaf of his Bible: "This book contains the mind of God, the state of man, the way of life, the doom of sinners, the happiness of believers. Read it to be wise. Believe it to be safe. Practice it to be holy. It gives light to direct you, food to support you, and comfort to cheer you. It is the traveler's map, the soldier's sword, the Christian's chart. Here Paradise is restored; Heaven is opened and the gates of Hell described. Christ is its Theme, our good its design and the glory of God its end."

Dr. Paul Tassell, the National Representative of the General Association of Regular Baptist Churches, is a man of today who loves the Word of God. He was saved at the age of seven, but when he was fourteen he was challenged by an evangelist to begin daily Bible reading and study. He earnestly desired to know God's will for his life, so he took the challenge seriously and from that time forward spent at least one hour each day in the Word.

The second in a family of six children, he soon found it was not always easy to find a time and place for his Bible study with so many brothers and sisters. He was determined, though, and for about three months went each day after school to the stair landing between the kitchen and basement of his home to meet with the Lord. He began in Genesis, read in a systematic way, and made up his mind to obey what he read in the Bible. God was even then, through His Word, preparing Paul Tassell for the important and challenging position he holds in our fellowship of churches today.

God's Word is the most wonderful Book in all the literature of the world. It contains the answer to every question of life, the solution to every problem man can face. Most important of all, this Book—God's written Word—points man to the Living Word, the Lord Jesus Christ, the only One through whom man can find forgiveness of sin and life eternal.

May

It's all over—that big event around which activities at our house have been revolving for about two years. What was it? The two-performance production of "Pilgrim's Progress" at Faith Baptist Bible College.

As I sat there each night, watching everyone appear looking as they were supposed to look and doing what they were supposed to do, it seemed like something of a miracle. I could not help but think of the untold hours of preparation on the part of untold numbers of people that made it happen.

Being married to the producer-pilgrim, it was hard for me to be objective about this—but I thought it was wonderful! I trust the presentation was a spiritual blessing and inspiration to "keep on in the Pilgrim Way."

Will any of us who saw it ever forget the fierce and *noisy* battle with Apollyon? Or that breathless moment when Pilgrim stepped through the veil into Heaven? Missionary Dorothy Adams wrote us that when she saw that, it was so real she wanted to cry out, "Wait for me—I'm coming, too!"

Costume headquarters were at the Doonan house

and you should have heard the whirrrr of sewing
machines—almost any hour of the day or night.
Mountains of used sheets created the picture of Heaven
for us as the white-robed celestial choirs appeared to
conclude the production with glorious alleluias.

With nearly 150 people in the cast and lots of moving
around, we were worried about the noise factor. Some
generous ladies made 150 pairs of double-knit slippers
and they did the trick. Thanks to them, the characters
moved softly and easily around the stage.

On the Tuesday after the performances I left Ankeny
bright and early and drove to Corning to spend the day
with the ladies of our Southwest regional churches. I
spoke twice, morning and afternoon. Their theme was
taken from 1 Corinthians 3:9—"SERVING TOGETHER—
WITH GOD!"

I told the ladies that day that we had just seen a living
example of this the previous weekend with so many, many
people using their unique abilities, from sewing to singing,
to make possible a presentation of the gospel message in
a unique way. We worked **with God,** and He blessed
abundantly. May He have all the glory!

June

It is spring again! That season of warm, balmy south breezes after a winter of cold, bitter north winds. That season of bird-song and bee-hum and blossoms on every bough. A sleek red cardinal is whistling in the neighborhood today, intent on finding a new place to set up housekeeping, I presume. The grass is lushly green, and my husband is busily putting a few seeds into the rain-softened ground. SPRING!

You have heard it said, haven't you, that in the spring a young man's fancy lightly turns to thoughts of—what the girls have been thinking of all winter!? Love, of course. It is wedding season again, and dozens of young couples find this their time of dreams come true.

As we see so many from FBBC who love the Lord and desire to serve Him establishing Christian homes, we rejoice with them and because of them. Our prayers go with them. May God bless them and use them in all their future days!

Speaking of weddings—here is a theme idea you ladies may want to file for future reference. On May 20th, it was my privilege to speak to the girls and ladies and their guests of Immanuel Baptist Church in Newton, Iowa. The theme for their annual mother-daughter event was "Olde-Fashioned Love." The tables were beautifully decorated as from an old-fashioned flower garden with fresh spring flowers and ferns.

Adding a special touch were programs in the form of pastel "brides" bouquets," one at each place. The programs were mimeographed in a circle and placed inside a round cover topped by a lace doily and tiny little cut-out flowers of every kind and color. Every bouquet was different, really beautiful, and represented lots and lots of work. A few streamers of ribbon at the bottom gave the illusion of a wedding bouquet.

Silk flower corsages were used as awards, and a unique feature was that they were presented just after the welcome, before the meal, so the winners were able to wear them for the entire evening.

After a lovely salad buffet (for which all recipes were available), we had wedding cake for dessert. It was the centerpiece on the head table and had been baked and decorated by one of the very creative and talented girls of the church. The spring flower motif was continued here with "sweet" blossoms of many hues sprinkled over its tiers. Yummy as well as pretty!

Many memories were relived as the teen-aged girls of the church gave us a fashion show of wedding dresses which had been worn by ladies of the congregation. The program was presented in the sanctuary and each came down the aisle as the narrator told how the original bride and her husband had met, some interesting facts about each, when and where they were married.

Of course, "yours truly" found lots to say on this theme and we all went away, I hope, more conscious of and grateful for the old-fashioned love of God—that perfect, best example of all love.

It had nothing to do with weddings, but I want to tell

you about another mother-daughter banquet because their theme was worth sharing and remembering. Think how much fun this one was to work out—"Christ, the Living Bread." The place was Walnut Park Baptist in Muscatine, Iowa.

Gingham-checked ribbon boxes in several pastel colors decorated the table corners as well as the lacquered loaves of real bread topped with tiny dried flowers which served as centerpieces on every table. The program cover was in the shape of a slice of bread with a tiny stalk of real wheat stapled across each one.

Our favors were hand-typed, stand-up recipe cards, each bearing a different bread recipe on the front (mine was zucchini bread) and a recipe for Scripture Cake on the back.

Awards were given to several ladies and these consisted of loaves of home-baked breads—different kinds—wrapped in plastic wrap and tied with gingham-checked ribbon, each with the recipe for it taped on the outside. The loaves were piled in two decorative baskets and made a pretty picture on the piano until they were used.

One of those loaves went to the lady present who had been saved the longest—seventy-two years! A little daughter saved only a few weeks won for the shortest time.

The ladies at this church did a wonderful job of working out the theme, and it was a blessing to end the evening we shared thinking about the Lord Jesus Christ, the One Who said so long ago, "I am the Bread of Life."

Remember the Southwest regional meeting in Corning that I wrote about last time? I wanted to tell you about the decorations. Everything was strawberries! And beautiful! You wonder why? Well, they were illustrating the truth of that passage concerning how one plants, another waters, but God gives the increase. I was especially impressed with the decorations on the luncheon tables—strawberry plants in all stages of growth. Very unusual and effective.

I hope these ideas will be a help and blessing to you. If you have any to share, I would love to hear from you.

Recently, I heard a missionary say that on the field they could always tell when it was summer in the United States—the "summer slump" in our churches made a difference in their work because fewer people were praying. Summer follows spring, you know, and it will soon be here. I hope you have a nice one, but let's all determine in our hearts not to "slump" this year. Let's keep praying fervently for God's servants the world around, and let's encourage God's servants right here (our pastors) by being faithful to our local churches during the summer months!

August

Have you ever had ants in your kitchen? As you read this question, I can just picture the grimaces and nodding of heads as you ladies recall the exasperation of such a discovery. We always ask, "Where in the world did they come from?" And sometimes it takes quite a while to find the answer to that question.

July 11th, this year, Mike and I had driven hard all day coming home from the last trip to Indiana University in Bloomington. We arrived late in the evening, weary and wanting to get to bed. As we unloaded our car, I stopped to set something on the kitchen counter. I noted a tiny, moving black speck . . . then another . . . then another. Suddenly I realized that my shower and bedtime would have to wait. I had ants in my kitchen!

Their size, shape and color were familiar to me. They were the "sweet-eaters." I called my husband to come and see what I had found. He smiled teasingly and said, "Aren't they cute?" Seeing I was in no mood for jokes, he quickly added, "Don't worry, I'll take care of them in no time."

A brief trip to the basement, some sweet and sticky goo poured on little squares of cardboard and set in their line of travel, and the doom of the little creatures was sealed. I breathed a sigh of relief, and could even smile myself a bit later when he called me to see what was happening.

If ants can be excited, these ants were. They had found the "feast" we had spread for them and they were gathering to enjoy it. Soon, every circle on the cardboard pieces was totally surrounded by ants crowded in as closely together as possible. A few were going, and still more were coming.

We stood and watched them and Mike called my attention to a curious thing. The ants that were "going" would stop by every ant they met "coming"; the two would touch noses, then both would hurry on. My husband explained the significance. "They are giving their friends a taste of the good thing they have found," he said. "That's how they communicate. That's how so many have found the feast."

We went to bed at last, and when we got up in the morning there was not an ant in sight. The little cardboard squares had been drained dry and the deadly poison had done its work. No longer did I have ants in my kitchen.

I thought about those ants. And I thought about the verse in God's Word which says we should go to the ants and learn from them. What did this experience have to teach me?

There was a very obvious lesson. I remembered how "excited" the little ants were about what they had found and how they stopped and told everyone they met in their own special way of communication. They literally gave a "taste" of the good thing and directions of how to find it.

As Christians, we have found something "good" and "sweet" that we can share with others. All about us are "hungry" souls. We meet them every day. Do we stop to give them a "taste" of the gospel and directions on where they can find more in the Word of God?

The little ants had no way of knowing that the thing which they shared with others would lead to their death. But we know for certain that what we have to share can save a soul from death and lead to life everlasting. Are we "excited" about that?

The psalmist exclaimed in Psalm 119:103, "How sweet are thy words unto my taste! Yea, sweeter than honey to my mouth!" Have you tasted God's Word today? Have you shared that sweetness with someone else? "Go to the ant . . . consider her ways and be wise."

September

It was one of those "heat wave" afternoons—Iowa's most unpleasant—with the temperature sizzling above ninety degrees and everything just dripping. The kind of afternoon when it is an effort just to breathe, and the best of folks complain, "It's not the heat, it's the humidity!"

On that particular afternoon, I was typing away in my office at FBBC where my boss was serving as interim president. I heard someone go into Mr. Brong's office (he was out of town) to use the phone. In just a few moments our adjoining door opened, and a familiar face that I hadn't seen for far too long appeared and the voice of an old friend spoke my name.

It was Bill (or should I say Dr. William?!) Fusco. He was on campus to speak to the Hiawatha Baptist Missions missionaries who gather here each summer for their annual conference.

We talked a moment before I asked Bill about his wife. He beamed. "She's here," he said, "right out there in the hall."

Needless to say, I went immediately "right out there in the hall." And I found Lorene. She was sitting in her wheelchair, patiently waiting for her husband, and not complaining one bit about the heat.

At one time, several years before, Lorene was not expected to live. They were located in California at that time, because Bill was Western Deputation Secretary for Baptist Mid-Missions. Lorene became very ill, then paralyzed, and was found to be suffering from a dreadful malignancy. It seemed there was no hope at all.

However, our God is able! As God's people around the world stormed the gates of Heaven in intercessory prayer, He answered with a miracle. Though still paralyzed, Lorene was able to be up, to travel with her husband on a limited basis, and to be an unbelievable blessing to Christians wherever she went. Her smile was just as radiant as ever, her outlook just as bright, her love for the Lord just as evident, and her desire to serve Him just as fervent.

As we visited there in the FBBC hallway, catching up on the time since we last saw one another, that dear lady must have said half a dozen times, "Oh, isn't God good?!" And she meant it. She was sincerely rejoicing in the goodness of her God.

We reminisced a little bit, remembering the year we met. The Fuscos, missionaries to Italy, were attending the FBBC missionary conference. They stayed in our home that weekend, and were a delight to our hearts. We have rarely experienced such wonderful, spiritual fellowship.

We learned during those days that Bill and Lorene were people of prayer. The four of us knelt together more than once, pouring out our hearts to the Lord in behalf of students who were seeking God's perfect will in their lives. God answered then, too.

On that hot afternoon Lorene Fusco sat in her wheel-chair and said, "Gladys, this illness has been good for me. I never before had enough time to spend in prayer, but now I can pray for hours and it's such a blessing."

She related how she prayed every day, by name, for those who serve at Denver Baptist Bible College where her husband is now president.

"And another thing," she said, "what a blessing it is to have students come to our home and have time to counsel with them without having to hurry." Her illness, which she says was "good" for her, has proven "good" for many others as well!

When I returned to my office after this challenging interlude, the heat no longer seemed to be such a problem. I was rejoicing in God's goodness, too—His goodness in sparing Lorene Fusco for an important and dedicated ministry of prayer and counseling—His goodness in using her testimony to speak to my heart and many hearts about the blessings of physical health and strength which we too often take for granted.

Lorene told me she reads my column, so right here in the JEWEL BOX I want to say thank you to this "precious jewel" of the Lord's for what she has meant to me. God bless you, Lorene, and give you happy years of rejoicing in His goodness and serving Him. We love you!

Note: Mrs. Fusco went Home to be with the Lord early in 1981, a few months after this article was originally published in "The Jewel Box."

October

She was a forlorn-looking little mite, walking slowly down the summer-hot Ankeny sidewalk in early August. As she approached our house, she saw Mike in the front yard trimming our hedge and stopped to watch. They talked a little bit over the whirr and snap of the electric trimmer before she asked that question that still tugs at our heartstrings when we think of it—"Will you be my new friend?"

Seems she had just moved here from another town and hadn't found any friends yet. There is really only one response one could give to such an appeal. Of course, Mike gave it. He assured her that he would be glad to be her new friend, and was rewarded by a happy twinkle in her pretty brown eyes and a wide smile revealing several gaps where baby teeth had been pulled. He asked her name and she told him. It was a pretty name, but the middle name, "Jewel," immediately caught my attention. I thought right away that she must someday find a place in my JEWEL BOX.

That conviction grew as the days went by and we learned more about *our* little friend, for by that time she had asked Mike if he had a wife and had requested to meet her. I, too, had become a "new friend."

This little "Jewel" was very frank, as most seven-year-olds are, and was quick to tell us that she didn't have a mommie—just a daddy. They lived together in an apartment nearby and she seemed very happy with the arrangement. She was eagerly looking forward to starting first grade in the fall.

One Sunday afternoon, soon after the beginning of this acquaintance and while my mother was visiting from Colorado, this little girl was chatting with us in our kitchen when she suddenly smiled and said, "Did you know that I'm saved? I have Jesus in my heart!"

She went on to explain that this had just happened recently, before she moved to our town, and she was disappointed that they had moved away from her "old" church before she had time to be baptized. That very evening she went to church with us, and sat on my lap watching wide-eyed as some children just a little older than herself followed the Lord in believer's baptism.

She went to Sunday School with us for several weeks, but we haven't seen her lately and we understand she has moved away, back to the town where she lived before. We miss her visits, and we find ourselves praying that she is going to her "old" church again and growing as a Christian.

Whenever we drive down that street where she lived, I think of that precious little "Jewel" the Lord sent our way who was unafraid and unashamed to witness of her salvation to three adults whom she had just met.

I look at the rows of apartment buildings on our Ankeny streets and wonder, too, how many people there are living in them who, like this little girl, need a friend but who, unlike her, won't go down the sidewalk looking for one.

Ladies, is there someone new in your town?

Someone who needs a friend? Someone you could invite to your church? Someone to whom you could witness?

May the Lord give us a concern for the people all about us who need not only our friendship, but an introduction to that Best Friend of all Who loved them and died for them, the Lord Jesus Christ. May we be willing to meet those needs!

November

Eight hundred miles one way is a long trip to take for just a weekend. We knew that when we started out, but we wouldn't have missed it for anything—that reunion of my husband's family in Pueblo, Colorado, on October 25th. Plans had been in the works for a long time. The event was first scheduled for summertime, but when a heart attack of one of Mike's older brothers cancelled that, someone suggested, "Why not in October, for Mom's birthday?" Then someone else, "And why not a surprise for her?"

We decided to use the cover of a wedding reception, admittedly a little bit late. Most of the family hadn't met Mary's new-husband-since-December, Bill. So Mom was told they would be coming home in the fall to have a party for this purpose, and all the family would try to make it, too.

Plans went full speed ahead. You can imagine how that was, with many of us involved in those plans hundreds of miles away from the reunion site and from one another. Lots of lengthy long-distance phone calls—Ma Bell should be grateful! And lots of letters—Uncle Sam should be, too!

110

From time to time, through those months of planning, things came up that made us wonder if one or another would be able to attend. Coordinating seven families timewise is no small matter, especially when they are located from Chicago to Washington state. But every crisis passed, confirmations were mailed in, transportation was arranged, and the last weekend in October finally arrived.

That Saturday dawned clear and crisp and cool—an ideal autumn day in colorful Colorado. There was a dusting of snow on the majestic mountains that rose deep blue against the horizon. We feasted our eyes and realized how much we missed them, even after all the years of being Midwesterners.

The celebration was held in the evening at Mom's church. Fellowship Hall was festive with crepe-paper streamers, balloons, a bountiful buffet table, a beautifully decorated cake and familiar faces everywhere. Friends and relations just came flocking in. Then, after everyone else was there, with a little extra flurry of excitement, the guest of honor arrived—Clara Iola Rank Doonan. She had come a long journey, too—all the way from October 25, 1900, and the little Iowa farm where she was born near Deep River.

How much Mom enjoyed having all of her seven children there with her to help celebrate her eightieth birthday. After all, it was the first time the whole family had been together for nineteen years!

There was talk and laughter, hugging and kissing, reminiscing and picture-taking, good food and fellowship in the Lord. We met some new family members and renewed acquaintances with old friends. We exclaimed over how much the nieces and nephews had grown, and we counted up how many great-grandchildren Mom has by now—twenty-five, I think. It was a truly exciting evening, one we will all remember for a long, long time.

As we drove back toward Iowa the next day, under cloudy skies and with raindrops pattering on the windshield, I thought about reunions. I thought about the fact that plans are already underway for another reunion, an even greater one than we had just attended—the reunion told about in God's Word which we will have in Heaven one day when we go to dwell forever with the Lord.

I found myself naming names—Mary and Bill, Doris and Jim, Russ and Patricia, Bill and Carolyn, Jim and Annette, Ruth and Jim, Ellen, Ann, Ron, Mary, Bill, Jimmy, Trish, Jay D., Janie, Rhonda, Michelle—on and on. And I found myself praying, "Lord, we want them ALL to be there on that day!"

It was so important to us that no one be absent from this reunion in Colorado. How much more important it is to us that no one be absent from that reunion in Heaven! And, as of right now, there may be some who are making no plans to attend.

How wonderful it is to realize that some faces absent from our reunions here on earth will be present when we gather up there. All who belong to the family of God through faith in the Lord Jesus Christ will be together for all eternity. That reunion is never going to end.

Most important of all—at that reunion, on that day, we are going to see a face we have never seen before—the face of God's Son, the One Who gave Himself to save us. The One Who made the great reunion possible. "And so shall we ever be with the Lord."

Ladies, have a joyful Thanksgiving, a merry Christmas, and a happy New Year, if the Lord tarries.

# January

Friday evening, December 5, the adults of Ankeny Baptist Church met together for their annual Christmas banquet. There were beautifully decorated tables in the traditional red and green. There was the soft glow of candlelight and the joyous sound of carols. There was special music and a challenging message around the theme, "Gifts for the Master." It was a lovely time of Christian fellowship!

One thing, though, was different about our banquet this year—the place in which it was held. A spirit of anticipation and excitement prevailed when the first announcement came that the event would be held in the "new" Des Moines Botanical Center. A meeting room had been rented for a very reasonable rate, and the food would be catered in.

The Des Moines Botanical Center is a very special place. Mike and I have been there perhaps half a dozen times since its opening, and we have placed it on our list as a must to share when we have out-of-town guests.

Particularly delightful is a visit on a sub-zero winter day. Stepping inside is just like stepping into summertime.

The air is near eighty degrees, the grass is green, trees and other plants are in full leaf, many in fragrant bloom. Luscious tropical fruits hang from the boughs, and there is the restful murmur of water falling over stones. It is truly a place of beauty.

This was our first visit in the evening, and it was even more beautiful than in the daytime. The air was pleasantly cool. Strong spotlights shone down from the center of the dome and tiny lights along the walkway directed our feet on the winding paths. The lights reflected in every pattern of the "big bubble" gave the illusion of walking along under millions of twinkling stars.

The west wall of our banquet room was all glass, overlooking the lighted skyline of the city of Des Moines. The east wall was all glass, looking into the gardens of the Center. Near holidays, special decorations are used, and on that December evening the Center was a glory of Christmas bloom with some five thousand poinsettia plants on display.

As we walked those paths observing the lush vegetation in that place and reading the little identifying markers provided for every living thing growing there, I began to think about those plants. The greatest percentage of them are in no way native to the climate and conditions of the Midwest. Many would undoubtedly die if planted outdoors in Iowa. However, brought together under that great transparent dome and given by the gardner just exactly what they need to survive, they flourish and blossom and bear fruit.

As a Christian, do you ever feel a little bit like one of those "hot-house plants"? Do you look about at the sin and growing wickedness of our world and think to yourself, "I don't belong here! The climate and conditions of today's world are too harsh! They will be the death of me!"

Do you read longingly in God's Book about that fair

land which shall some day be our eternal home—a land where only those who know and love Christ shall dwell—a land where there will be no more sin, pain or darkness?

It is, of course, good and right that we should feel this way. And yet we should not become, as someone has wisely put it, "so heavenly minded we are no earthly good." We are not "hot-house plants." We are in the world, planted by the hand of the Master Gardner just where He wants us.

While we are here, we should do all we can to conquer sin, to relieve pain, to dispel the darkness. As we are faithful and obedient and submissive to our Lord and the teaching of His Word, the climate and conditions of the world will only cause us to grow stronger as Christians, to blossom more beautifully, to bear sweeter fruit.

As we look ahead to the coming days and weeks and months of the new year, we are perhaps fearful of what they may bring. We need to remember that our Master Gardener, God Himself, is in control and He knows just exactly what we need to survive. These things He has provided freely for us.

We are blessed to live in a free land where we are privileged to meet with others of like precious faith to worship and fellowship. We have the Bible in our homes and in our hands to guide us and nourish us in our Christian life. We have the awesome blessing of access to God in prayer.

There is a little phrase we hear every so often that seems most appropriate as we close our visit today—a "jewel" for your "jewel box"—**Bloom where you're planted!** I like that.

Your place may not be sheltered and beautiful as in the Des Moines Botanical Center, but it is God's place for you. And my challenge to you (and myself) for the new year is this—"BLOOM [FOR HIM] WHERE YOU'RE PLANTED!"

February

Good morning, ladies! Today it is two below zero outdoors, and I can hear the crunch of cars going by on the snow-packed street. The Iowa winter has given up on mimicking spring, and it looks and feels like February. Come on into my cozy yellow kitchen for a nice, warm visit.

See what I got for Christmas—there, on the top of that little bookcase? You know what it is, don't you? A new recipe box! You can tell just by looking at it that it is a "one-of-a-kind original," and how do you like that shine? It has seven coats of hand-rubbed finish!

Yes, it's maple—very Early American. Of course, the back is redwood—and isn't that design unique? Remind you of a violin? There's a reason for that. Mike says it is to thank me for the 102-year-old violin I gave him for our anniversary in December. He has wanted one all his life, and is having more fun learning to play it.

Didn't I tell you he made my "treasure box?" I call it that, not for the recipes it contains but because I am going to "treasure" it all the rest of my life. I especially like this tiny porcelain knob that lifts the slanting lid and this little groove for a pencil on top.

116

And all that room! The two compartments will hold a double set of 3x5 cards. Now I won't have to pinch my fingers or tear a card in getting one out of that little, jammed box I used to use. I just love my Christmas present!

With a new recipe box, you know what I have been doing, don't you? I have been sorting my recipes. It's lots of fun and I've found some I had forgotten I had. Now I'd like to try them all over again.

You know, some people guard their recipes and keep them a secret forever. Not me! I like to share, and I thought I'd share one of my very favorites with you this morning. I got it from a friend many years ago, and I think it is the best coffeecake in the world. Of course, served with a dab of whipped topping it makes a great dessert, too.

This is called simply Heath Bar Cake, and it is what I always make for the Council of Ten and the State Youth Committee when they meet in our office. Pastor Bernie Payne says it is "like a drum with a hole in it—it can't be beat!"

HEATH BAR CAKE

Combine: 2 cups flour, 2 cups brown sugar, 1 stick oleo or butter.

Mix until crumbs. Save out one cup of the crumbs. Stir into the remainder: 1 unbeaten egg, 1 teaspoon vanilla, 1 cup milk with 1 teaspoon soda dissolved in it.

Pour batter into a greased oblong cake pan, sprinkle with reserved crumbs, nut pieces and 4 crushed Heath candy bars. Bake at 350° 30-35 minutes.

There's another recipe I want to share with you. I found it in my scrapbook and I think you will like it.

RECIPE FOR A HAPPY LIFE

Take a large quantity of CHEERFULNESS and let it simmer without stopping. Put with it a brimming portion of KINDNESS, and add a full measure of THOUGHTS FOR OTHER PEOPLE. Mix in

117

SYMPATHY and flavor with the essence of CHARITY. Stir well and then carefully strain off any grains of SELFISHNESS. Let the whole be served with a sauce of LOVE and generous helpings of the FRUIT OF THE SPIRIT.

The other day I looked up the word "recipe" in my dictionary and found something interesting. One meaning given by Mr. Webster is "a means prescribed for producing a desired result." Then it occurred to me that if we use that meaning, the Bible is just full of recipes.

For instance, if the result you desire for your life is direction from the Lord, you can find the "recipe" in Proverbs 3:5, 6. "Trust in the Lord with all thine heart; and lean not unto thine own understanding. In all thy ways acknowledge him, and he shall direct thy paths."

I found the recipe for perfect peace in Isaiah 26:3 and the recipe for the very desires of your heart is in Psalm 37:4.

This is an interesting and rewarding new way of looking at God's Word. I challenge you, ladies—let's all see how full we can fill our "Scriptural recipe boxes" during the coming year!

March

Late every Tuesday afternoon, a young boy comes along the sidewalk in front of our house and pitches over the hedge a little paper, rolled up and secured with a rubber band. It is the type of advertising sheet commonly called a "shopper."

I usually take the time to read it, trying to find a way to save a few cents on the grocery bill or other items we need, because in this day of inflation every penny counts.

Not only does the shopper include ads from the stores and shops of our community, but there are classified ads offering items for sale, houses for rent, services available. Once in a while I will glance idly through these, too.

Last week, in doing that, something caught my eye. It was in a help wanted ad for someone to take a position in a certain office. The usual information was given regarding hours, pay scale and application procedure.

In regard to qualifications, there was this statement: "Must be a self-starter." I chuckled when I read that, but I kept thinking about it all evening. I work in an office and I know what that means. Do you? A poet once defined the term very well in these brief lines.

Don't wait for someone to tell you
What needs to be done or just why;
The world always gives its best blessings
To the one who observes with quick eye;
Whose hand goes out on occasion
To welcome, to lift and to guide;
Who's always delighted to carry,
And not always seeking to ride.
Don't expect someone to crank you,
To explain, or to give you the cue.
What the world needs is self-starters,
Who see, then get busy and do!

How about you? Would you qualify for that job? Are you a self-starter? How about in your "job" as a Christian woman, wife, homemaker, mother, church member—are you a self-starter there? Do you realize how important it is that you are?

The Christian home is not like the worldly home. At least, it should not be. This is very clearly your responsibility. You set the tone. You are the one who can make your home a place filled with LOVE and JOY and PEACE and ORDER.

Being a self-starter will help you keep your home neat and clean and inviting—a haven for your family when they come in from the daily harshness of a world that is no friend to grace. A self-starter is the kind of woman who sets priorities in her life and then honors them—the kind of woman who digs right in and does the disagreeable, monotonous chores without complaining; the kind of woman who doesn't have to hear her child say, "Mom, don't I have any clean socks?" or her husband say, "Isn't my shirt ironed?" to stir her to action; the kind of woman who is thankful for the home God has given her, no matter how humble, and is a good steward in caring for it and those who live there; the kind of woman who knows

120

her home has great potential as a testimony for the Lord in her neighborhood.

A Christian mother who is a self-starter will recognize and rejoice in the wonderful blessing of being a parent. She will teach her little ones about the Lord every day of her life, beginning even before they are able to walk and talk. She will take them to God's house but will not leave the responsibility for their spiritual learning to the pastor or the Sunday School teacher. She will not wait for problems to come before she begins to solve them. She will spend time with her children each day, having fun with them and building a line of communication that will be strong enough to withstand the difficult teen years ahead. She will realize the challenge described in these lines from an unknown poet.

> There are little eyes upon you, and they're
>   watching night and day;
> There are little ears that quickly take in
>   every word you say;
> There are little hands all eager to do
>   everything you do;
> There's a little one just waiting to grow up
>   to be like you!

She will consistently and consciously seek to be the kind of example they need.

In the church, a Christian woman who is a self-starter can be a great blessing. She will be the kind of person who takes the initiative to invite her neighbors, greet the stranger, encourage the pastor and his wife, visit the sick and sorrowing, help the needy in a practical way, discourage gossip, heal hurt feelings, be a friend to everyone both young and old, and PRAY.

Well, there they are—the thoughts that little word "self-starter" brought into my mind. I want to be one in every area of my life. Do you? There are times when I feel I am not making much headway, but the Lord is faithful to help and encourage and give me the desire to go on. It is a desire which I believe is pleasing to Him.

A verse from His Word which has been a blessing to me is 1 Corinthians 15:58. "Therefore, my beloved brethren, be ye stedfast, unmoveable, always abounding in the work of the Lord, forasmuch as ye know that your labour is not in vain in the Lord."

May

My April birthday this year dawned dark and rainy. It didn't dampen my spirits, though, because some friends brightened my day by helping me celebrate (?) being another year older. At 8:00 that morning a car pulled into our driveway, and I ran out to be greeted by a chorus of "happy birthdays" from Leah, Elnora, Shirley and "the other Gladys."

What fun it was to drive to a Des Moines restaurant where they treated me to breakfast! My omelette was yummy! Then we went on a shopping spree—and that is why I am telling you all of this.

One of the things we bought that day was a clock for the reception room of the state office.

I dislike making decisions that have to do with spending someone else's money—in this case, the Association's. I find myself worrying for fear my choice might not please others. But, as you can see, I solved that problem rather nicely this time by letting ladies of a couple of different churches do the decision-making.

It was nice they chose the very clock I had my eye on—all five of us were in perfect agreement. Now you will have to stop by our state office sometime to see our new "timepiece," and if you don't like it—well, I can at least share the blame with someone else.

The clock is an Elgin Quartz Regulator. That last word probably tells you its styling. It is "Early American" looking, even though with the latest technology of the industry it runs on two little D-size flashlight batteries. It has clear, black numerals and even a little brass pendulum that swings smoothly back and forth with never a hesitation or break in the rhythm. Now, when folks visit our office they will no longer have to ask the secretary, "What time is it?"

What time is it? I wonder if you could count the times you have heard those words. It is a question most of us ask or answer several times every day of our lives. The things we do are governed by time. We have a certain time to get up, a certain time to eat our meals, a certain time to visit the dentist or hairdresser, a certain time to go to work, a certain time to go to bed. We ask, "What time is it?" so we will not be too early or too late.

What time is it? We do well to ask that question in regard to our spiritual lives as well. God's Word is the "timepiece" which has the answer to our question.

If you have somehow picked up a state paper and are reading the JEWEL BOX and yet have never asked the Lord Jesus Christ into your heart and life, God's Word says that for you it is *time to be saved.* Second Corinthians 6:2 says, ". . . behold, now is the accepted time; behold, now is the day of salvation."

God wants to save you from your sin. "He is not willing that any should perish." All you have to do is admit you are a sinner, believe Jesus died to save you and that He is able to do it, then come to Him just as you are and tell Him so. He has promised that no one who comes to Him for salvation will be refused.

If you already know the Lord, and I am sure most of you do, God's Word tells you what time it is, too. For the

Christian it is *time to serve!* Ephesians 5:15-17 gives us this message: "See then that ye walk circumspectly, not as fools, but as wise, redeeming the time, because the days are evil. Wherefore be ye not unwise, but understanding what the will of the Lord is."

As I sit here writing to you today, the calendar before me says that this is the first day of May. I find myself asking in bewilderment, "Where did April go?" Time goes by so swiftly and there is so much that needs to be done for the Lord. That is why we need to be "redeeming the time."

I don't know who wrote it, but this little poem says it all. When you wonder "What time is it?" remember these words.

Two little lines I heard one day,
As I walked along my usual way,
And they rang in my ears again and again,
Repeating in solemn, sweet refrain,
"Only one life, 'twill soon be past;
Only what's done for Christ will last."

"Only one life!" The still, small voice
Gently allures to the better choice,
Bidding me never let selfish aims
Overshadow the Saviour's claims.
"Only one life, 'twill soon be past;
Only what's done for Christ will last!"

Give me, Saviour, a purpose deep,
In joy or sorrow Thy trust to keep;
And so, through trouble and care and strife,
Glorify Thee in my daily life.
"Only one life, 'twill soon be past;
Only what's done for Christ will last!"

WHAT TIME IS IT? TIME TO GET BUSY!

June

April 28, my friend Mary Kilburn and I had an adventure. It was scary, but it was also another proof that God answers prayer and watches over His own children.

Many months ago I had received an invitation from the ladies at What Cheer, Iowa, to join them for the day of their Southeast-Central regional ladies' meeting. I was, of course, honored and delighted to be asked. Since my husband doesn't like for me to drive any great distance alone, I invited Mary to go along for the ride and what I was sure would be a day of wonderful Christian fellowship.

It wasn't raining when we left Ankeny, but the farther east we got, the darker the sky. First some sprinkles, then rain, finally some thunder and lightning and a real cloudburst. When we turned off Interstate 80 onto Highway 21 South, it hit us full force—driving, blinding rain and pounding hail. I would have pulled off but I couldn't see the shoulder. We had prayed before leaving and I was praying then, in my heart, as I drove.

Isn't the Lord good? He sent a truck along in front of us. I found if I could stay quite close to him, I could follow his little red tail light, and we got safely to our destination.

As we walked in the door of the church out of the sprinkles, one of the ladies from What Cheer laughed and said, "I suppose it is our fault—our theme today is "There Shall Be Showers of Blessing!"

And there were! The pastor's wife and her ladies had planned and prepared such a lovely day for us. I spoke twice—once rather extemporaneously in the morning when I was expecting about ten minutes and was given fifty-five! Then again in the afternoon.

Because I promised many of the ladies there that day that I would reprint a little poem I used, here it is just for them. It has a message for all of us.

> If all that we say in a single day,
> With never a word left out,
> Were printed each night in clear
>   black and white,
> It would make strange reading,
>   no doubt.
>
> And then just suppose, ere our eyes
>   we would close,
> We must read the whole record through;
> Wouldn't we sigh, and wouldn't we try
> A whole lot less talking to do?
>
> I certainly think that many a kink
> Would be smoother in life's tangled
>   thread
> If half that we say in a single day
> Were forever left unsaid.

Spring brings not only our regional ladies' meetings, but mother-daughter events in churches all across the state. I like to report on the ones I attend because there are always so many good ideas used that might be of help to another group another year.

It was my privilege to speak at four this year—three

evening banquets and an early-afternoon luncheon. What a delight to meet and fellowship with these ladies!

Two of the churches used my own mother-daughter program, *Sugar and Spice,* and it was fun to see the ways they worked it out. The programs were pretty and could be used with any theme. One of the churches made a lace-trim oval on the front of their cover, and inside it were two "sun-bonnet girls" (big and little) cut from contrasting-color gingham check fabric and trimmed with bits of lace. The other church made the whole cover of pink and white gingham check fabric, and decorated these with mother-daughter silhouettes. Both of these churches had a nice salad buffet and one had a hot meat dish in addition. In both places the men and boys helped with serving and clean-up.

It was a blessing to think again about the "sugar and spice," sweetness and zest the Lord can put into the lives of those of us who belong to Him!

There was the sweetest little poem printed in one program—so sweet I wanted to share it with you. It is called "A Lovely Surprise" and was written by Kay Andrew.

> Life has started all over for me,
> The young years of happiness
> Have come again in a sweeter form
> Than a mother could ever guess,
> The love and devotion I gave my child
> I thought I could give no other,
> But life held a lovely surprise for me—
> This year I became a grandmother!

The ladies of still another church held their banquet at a restaurant and I think about seventy to seventy-five attended. Their theme was unique—"Ministry of Motherhood." You may notice that an acrostic on these words spells MOM! They used an old-fashioned decorating scheme of hearts and flowers and had the cutest favors I've seen.

Beside each place was a single homemade mint that formed the center of a lovely flower. Pop bottle caps had been sprayed gold, along with their inside cork or cardboard liners. Scalloped circles were cut of rainbow-colored tissue paper and five layers pressed into the center of the cap. The liner was then pressed back in to hold the petals and the mint laid in the center. Wish you could have seen them blooming all over the tables!

Every part of the program at this banquet was very well prepared and presented and I was especially impressed with their special music. A beautiful duet and two numbers by a ladies' trio just thrilled my heart.

Saturday, May 2, was a beautiful, sunny day and my husband drove me to Montezuma for their mother-daughter luncheon. It was spring inside as well as outside that day because their theme was "Daisies Do Tell!" Can you guess what they used for decorating?

Several ladies and girls took part in a fashion show of home-sewn garments, and we all enjoyed that very much. We wound up the afternoon's activities by considering some of the things I have learned from the daisies in my garden, and we found that "Daisies Do Tell!"

August

Do you like to sew? It is one of my favorite pastimes and my only complaint is that I don't have enough time for it. Mike has fixed me the loveliest room in our basement where my sewing machine is always out, always waiting for me to come. The room has white walls, a white ceiling and fluorescent lighting, and the nicest thick, soft, red carpet a person could hope to dig his toes into. My writing desk is there. The new typewriter I have on order will be there. My ironing board is always up and on the table is my sewing machine. I tell Mike it is my favorite room in the house—that I am tempted just to go down there and "be a hermit."

Hardly ever do I go down into my basement or sit down at my sewing machine without thinking of a Bible study I heard when I was a teenager growing up in Colorado. The pastor of our church, on that particular Wednesday night, asked us to turn to the book of Philippians and he read verses 12 through 16 of the second chapter.

"Wherefore, my beloved, as ye have always obeyed, not as in my presence only, but now much more in my

130

absence, work out your own salvation with fear and trembling. For it is God which worketh in you both to will and to do of his good pleasure. Do all things without murmurings and disputings: That ye may be blameless and harmless, the sons of God, without rebuke, in the midst of a crooked and perverse nation, among whom ye shine as lights in the world; Holding forth the word of life; that I may rejoice in the day of Christ, that I have not run in vain, neither laboured in vain."

Our pastor was quick to explain that working out one's own salvation was not salvation by good works, as some falsely teach. Christ purchased our salvation on the cross of Calvary, and the only way we can receive it is by putting our faith and trust in Him as personal Savior, and being cleansed of our sin through His blood. This verse means, rather, that after we have received salvation from Him as a free gift, we go to work to make of our Christian life something beautiful and winsome and honoring to Christ.

Then he used the illustration I have never forgotten. He said it was something like a woman sewing. She goes out to the store, buys a piece of material and a pattern, gets some thread and a zipper and maybe some trim, and comes home with a new dress! Yes, it is a dress. It is all there; it just isn't "worked out" yet!

Remembering this, I went to the fabric store the other day where they were having a sale. I came home with a big bag and showed my husband my bargains. I held up a pretty piece of interlock knit I had picked up for less than half-price and said, "Look, dear, a new dress!" He laughed with me then, because he was a teenager in that same church and heard that same Bible study. It has afforded us much food for thought over the years and both of us are still trying every day to "work out our salvation."

Sometimes in my sewing I make mistakes. I bungle a seam or make a crooked hem, which gives me a finished product that I am not very proud to claim. It comes because of my own carelessness. I don't follow the pattern carefully or closely enough.

How often it is like that in my Christian life, too. I bungle an opportunity for service. I get my priorities all crooked. And I wonder if my Savior looks at me and isn't very proud to claim me even though I am His own child. It's all my own fault. The Word is my pattern—Christ, the Living Word; the Bible, the written Word. I just have not followed my Pattern carefully or closely enough.

I know many of you ladies are busy right now with your fall sewing. You're making little dresses and trousers so your children will be warm and well-dressed as they go to school through the winter.

As you sit at your sewing machine these days, I challenge you to meditate on these thoughts. As you follow the pattern for the little clothes you are making, I challenge you to consider how closely you are following the Pattern for your Christian life as you "work out your own salvation" day by day.

Let's strive to make our Christian lives our very best "creation." Let's pray that the Lord will help us to become women of inner beauty and sweetness, eagerly sharing by lip and by life the good news of this salvation we already have, but which we need to "work out."

# September

On a hot summer Sunday evening in July, I sat in the pleasant living room of the parsonage of one of our churches in western Iowa. Next door in the church, my husband and the other two members of the Laudamus Trio were preparing a concert for the evening service. I was visiting with the pastor's wife and their very young son, who is a dark-haired little charmer.

They had returned recently from a trip to the GARBC national conference. On that trip the little boy got some new toys. He was showing them to me and showing me how they worked while I sipped lemonade. Suddenly, he jumped up and said, "Now I want to show you my daddy's new toy!" He ran to a nearby bookcase, stood on tippy-toes to reach the top, and brought something I had never seen before and dropped it in my lap.

It was a plastic cube made up of tiny squares, nine to a side, in six different colors—red, blue, green, yellow, white and orange. I found that these little squares could be rotated vertically or horizontally. The object of the puzzle is to return the little squares to their original position of a solid color on each face of the cube.

Sounds easy, doesn't it? It is not! We bought our own Rubik's Cube soon after and have not solved it yet. It was devised by a Hungarian architect, and we are told there are over three billion combinations which can be formed, but only one solution.

An article in the May 1981 *Reader's Digest* tells of a twenty-five-year-old Frenchman who claims he can return the cube to its original state in about thirty-two seconds. A sixteen-year-old English boy says he can do it in forty seconds.

Having played with it a bit myself, I find these hard to believe. I think this puzzle has the potential of driving one mad!

Puzzles are fun, especially when you don't have anything else to do. Many of you mothers may find yourselves in this position today, with the kids back in school and the house uncannily quiet. I recommend Rubik's Cube. However, you may not have one or be able to find one nearby. Therefore, I decided I would include a couple of puzzles in my column this month just for you. I guarantee they are not as difficult as Rubik's Cube!

Can you find them? In these re<u>marks</u> are hidden the names of fifteen books of the Bible. It's a real lulu. Kept me looking so hard for facts I missed the revelation. I was in a jam especially since the names were not capitalized. The truth will come to numbers of our readers. To others it will be a real job. For all it will be a most fascinating search. Yes, there will be some easy to spot; others hard to judge. So we admit it usually results in loud lamentations when we can't find them. One lady says she brews coffee while she puzzles over it. One book is underlined to help you find the other fourteen.

And, how about this next one?

WHO AM I?

Adam, God made out of dust,
But thought it best to make me first,
So I was made before man
To answer God's most holy plan.
A living being I became
And Adam gave to me my name.
I from his presence then withdrew,
And more of Adam never knew.
I did my Maker's law obey
Nor ever from it went astray.
Thousands of miles I go in fear
But seldom do on earth appear.
For purpose wise which God did see,
He put a living soul in me.
A soul from me God did claim,
And took from me the soul again.
So when from me the soul had fled,
I was the same as when first made.
And without hands, or feet, or soul,
I travel on from pole to pole.
I labor hard by day, by night;
To fallen man I give great light.
Thousands of people, young and old,
Will by my death great light behold.
No right or wrong can I conceive,
The Scriptures I cannot believe.
Although my name is therein found,
They are to me an empty sound.
No fear of death doth trouble me,
Real happiness I'll never see;
To Heaven I shall never go,
Nor shall I go to Hell below.
Now, when these lines you slowly read,

Go search your Bible with all speed,
For that my name is written there
I do honestly to you declare.

(This puzzle was written by a lady in California in response
to an offer from a gentleman in Philadelphia that he would
pay anyone $1,000 who could write a puzzle he could not
solve. He failed to do so and paid the $1,000. The answer
is one word and appears only four times in the Bible.)

So, there you are. That will give you something to do
in those spare, quiet moments whenever (and if ever!)
they come. Have fun, and I will plan to print the solutions
to these two next month. If you want the solution to
Rubik's Cube, you will have to order the 66-page booklet
which gives it to you. The address comes with the Cube.

There is another puzzle, too, that you might spend
some time thinking about and trying to solve this month.
It is one, though, for which I cannot print the solution. It is
a puzzle none of us will understand until we get to Glory.
Why did God the Father love sinful folks like us so much
that He was willing to give His own dear Son to save us? It
is a continual marvel, but a wonderful truth. Take some
time today just to thank God for His great love!

October

Do you ever PROCRASTINATE? That big word is, of course, found under the "p's" in Mr. Webster's dictionary and he tells us it means "to postpone; to put off intentionally and habitually." You know what it means—putting off until tomorrow something you should be doing today!

I must admit, once in a while I find within myself a tendency to procrastinate. During this past year, I procrastinated about getting my eyes examined. The calendar said it was time. My eyes told me it needed to be done. But, somehow, there just never was a "right" time to call for the appointment, to "waste time" waiting in a doctor's office, to pay the sizable sum I knew my new glasses would cost. So, I put it off.

It worried me a little bit that I had to squint so hard to see things any distance away—things like highway signs when driving—but I had no problem when something was close enough. So, on Sunday I would adjust my hymnal a notch nearer my nose, mentally reminding myself that I *must* do something about getting my eyes checked.

Monday would come, back to work, another hectic

week with no time for "extras"—and the procrastination went on.

Then one day a friend mentioned to me that she needed to get her eyes checked. I said emphatically, "I do, too!" She had heard of a good doctor in a nearby town and suggested, "Why don't I call and get appointments for both of us on the same day; then we can go together?" This solved my problem, and one sunny May afternoon we walked through the door of the clinic where that doctor was located.

It wasn't a bad ordeal at all, and I was relieved to find nothing drastically wrong with my eyes—just too many birthdays! I received a prescription for new glasses, but the doctor made a mistake! He told me they weren't really too much of a change from my old ones! Oh, oh! You know what happened, don't you? That gave me an excuse to procrastinate again, this time about getting the prescription filled.

However, I finally did it! I have new glasses and, even though they are a couple of months old now, I am still not used to the wonderful improvement they have made in my vision. I wonder why on earth I waited so long to get that eye exam!

As I recently thought about this whole succession of events and how well I am seeing these days, I found myself wondering if my spiritual "vision" was as good as my physical vision now. I came to the conclusion that perhaps we Christians need an "exam" periodically in this regard as well as the other.

Once in a while, something my Sunday School teacher or my pastor or a special speaker at the state ladies' meeting says makes me wonder if I am "seeing" things as I ought to. Is my "vision" a little dim? A little blurred? Am I so wrapped up in those things which are "close" to me—my own little concerns—that I fail to "see" clearly the needs of others? Am I truly aware of how many, many

138

needy souls there are down the road a ways, or on the other side of the world?

This is exactly what Jesus was talking about in John 4:35 when He said to His followers, "Behold, I say unto you, Lift up your eyes and look on the fields; for they are white already to harvest."

I am one of His followers today. Probably you are as well. His command to us is the same one. He wants us to "lift up our eyes and look," too. We will not be concerned if our spiritual "vision" is faulty. But when we "see" clearly, we will get busy and do what we can about meeting the need.

Say, how is your spiritual "vision?" Do you need an "I Exam"? If the answer is yes, don't procrastinate!

By the way, we have a little bit of unfinished business from last month, don't we? How did you get along with my puzzles? I promised you the answers, and here they are. The answer to the "WHO AM I?" poem is *whale*—specifically, the one that swallowed Jonah. And the underlined letters in the following paragraph will show you all of the fifteen books of the Bible hidden there.

In these re<u>marks</u> are hidden the names of fifteen books of the Bible. It's a real lu<u>lu. Kept</u> me loo<u>king</u> <u>so</u> hard for <u>facts</u> that I missed the <u>revelation</u>. I was in a <u>jam</u> especially since the names were not capitalized. The <u>truth</u> will come to <u>numbers</u> of our readers. To others it will be a real <u>job</u>. For all it will be <u>a most</u> fascinating search. Yes, <u>there</u> will be some easy to spot; others hard to <u>judge</u>. So we admit <u>it usually</u> results in loud <u>lamentations</u> when we can't find them. One lady says <u>she brews</u> coffee while she puzzles over it.

139

# November

One day this past week, I drove to Des Moines to do some shopping. The first store I entered was all in a turmoil. The stationery supplies were not in their normal spot, and I wandered about wondering where to find the envelopes I needed to replenish my depleted supply at home.

I had to step over some things and dodge others and I noticed that a few counters, evidently newly emptied, were already being refilled with items from boxes that crowded the aisles beside them. Busy clerks bustled around creating the new displays. Suddenly, I realized what was happening. They were getting ready for Christmas—and October wasn't even quite gone yet!

As I stood looking at the sparkling decorations, the stacks of foil-covered boxes of every size and shape, the big bags of beautifully colored ribbons, I was reminded that we are once again approaching that special season in which gifts play so large a part. I love giving gifts, and mentally began making a list of people I wanted to remember.

We who are Christians delight in this season as we recall again, in a special way, that God so loved the world that He gave! He gave the most perfect gift for any occasion ever when He gave His Son to save a world lost in sin. Romans 6:23 tells us, ". . . the gift of God is eternal life through Jesus Christ our Lord." How wonderful that all who believe may have that life, that salvation, that gift!

There is a Christmas poem by an unknown author that I like very much. It tells of God's gift and it goes like this:

> God did not use a silvery box
> Or ribbons green and red.
> He laid His Christmas Gift to man
> Within a manger bed.
>
> No silken cord was used to bind
> The Gift sent from above,
> 'Twas only wrapped in swaddling bands
> And bound in cords of love.
>
> There was no evergreen to which
> His precious Gift was tied;
> Upon a bare tree on a hill
> His Gift was hung—and died.
>
> 'Twas taken down from off the tree
> And laid beneath the sod,
> But even death could not destroy
> The precious Gift of God.
>
> With mighty hand He lifted Him
> From out the stony grave.
> FOREVERMORE, FOR EVERY MAN,
> A LIVING GIFT GOD GAVE!

How can we help but join the apostle in his exclamation, "Thanks be unto God for his unspeakable gift" (2 Cor. 9:15).

Did you ever hear the story of the ladies who met for lunch one day to celebrate with their friend her baby's first birthday? As they ate and talked and laughed, an acquaintance stopped by their table and was told of the special occasion. She looked around the little circle in bewilderment and then asked, "The baby's birthday? But where is the baby?" The mother giggled and said, "Oh, I couldn't bring the baby. He's too little to celebrate!"

Christmas is the time we celebrate our Savior's birthday. This year, let's not celebrate without Him. Let's include Him in every plan and let's put His name at the top of our gift list and makes our first, best gift the one we give to Him! Most of all He wants our hearts, our lives, our obedience, our faithfulness. If we give Him these gifts, we will be able to serve Him well.

Of course, we will be giving gifts to others we love, too. Perhaps these few practical ideas may be of help to you.

Some people give *gift certificates* from stores at Christmastime, but have you ever considered giving gift certificates you make yourself, which only you can redeem? One birthday my husband gave me an envelope of these, and it was one of the most cherished gifts I ever received. Each certificate was for something different; one was for ten walks with him whenever and wherever I chose; another was for five times of eating out; still another for ten times of his doing dishes for me; others were for kisses and equally valuable items, but all were very special. These certificates were good for one year and I had fun claiming them just when they were most needed.

This same idea can be used by you with elderly friends or relatives. Give certificates for such things as driving them places, doing errands for them, a coffee break when they are especially lonely (with you bringing the refreshments). Give young couples certificates for baby-sitting, thus providing a special evening out. The ideas are endless.

142

Along the same line, why not give the children you love the gift they would like best of all—some of your time? Call them *time capsules.* Mark on tiny papers the name of the gift—a trip to the zoo, a walk in the park, a treat at the ice cream store together—roll these up and stuff them in empty capsules you can get from your druggist. A bottle of them to last over a year's time would be unique, and would make some little person wonderfully happy!

Too often even we Christians get caught up in the game of spending too much "plastic money" during December, and worrying about paying bills in January. Expensive gifts are not necessary. They can be nice if they are thoughtfully chosen, but even better is a gift of yourself!

It was Martin Luther who said, "The heart of the giver makes the gift dear and precious!" To give a perfect gift, you may need to spend very little money if you are creative and give something of yourself. Just remember, ladies—

> It's not what you'd do with a million,
> If that should be your lot,
> But it's what you're doing here and now
> With the dollar that you've got!

Merry Christmas! Happy Gift-Giving!!